The Infinite Circle of the Soul

A Non-Religious View of Spirituality

Mike Hain

ECSM Publishing—Aurora, CO
ISBN: 978-1-7365591-0-9
Library of Congress Control Number: 2021902171
Title: The Infinite Circle of the Soul
Author: Mike Hain
Digital distribution | 2020
Paperback | 2020

Published in the United States by New Book Authors Publishing

Dedication

For my kids, family, and all of the writers to whom their words made their way into my life

"The forces of nature will open up and present the possibilities. It's up to you to embrace them or not."

—Me

Table of Contents

Preface

For the longest time, I've had a strong desire to write a book. Next to being a successful musician, that was a dream of mine. Always thinking it was one of the greatest accomplishments one could achieve, I hoped that one day I would be someone who would conquer such an enormous goal. I truly wish that the circumstances which led me to write this book would have not existed, however, I do honestly believe that it was for the best and I am extremely thankful for the experience. It has been said over and over throughout the years that art, whether that be painting, music, writing, or any other artistic piece, would not have been created without unhappiness, struggle, or heartache. Sometimes beauty is born from our most difficult experiences.

When I was much younger (high school and college to be exact) I loved writing. It was an outlet for my pre-adulthood, dream-filled mind and also was just plain fun for me. As I got older and life filled with other "necessary" tasks, it seemed to fall by the wayside. It was only in the last few years and due to unhappiness that I began the writing aspect of my life again. I guess I started writing again primarily to vent my feelings and to leave behind my thoughts just in case tomorrow I wasn't around anymore. Sappy and sadly romantic I know, but that's how a writer thinks sometimes.

When my journey began, however many months ago, I had no idea where it would take me. There were days it took me absolutely nowhere but down a hole of sadness. Thankfully, my road of sadness led me from one positive idea to the next and to eventually writing this book. If it wasn't for my amazing kids, family, and all of the wonderful writers' books that found their way into my hands, I don't know where I would have ended up. I will forever be grateful for those people and their words.

I hope that you enjoy reading this book as much as I did writing it.

Two-Parter

The soul. What exactly is it? I believe that each and every one of us possesses a soul. In truth, it is our true essence or self. You are your soul and your soul is you. Our soul needs knowledge to grow and become whole. For this to be possible, each of our soul's passes from lifetime to lifetime gathering knowledge through life lessons. There are many ways to attain this wholeness. The first of these is prayer/meditation. This is an extremely crucial factor in the progression of our soul. In my opinion, there are two facets and reasons for prayer. Keep in mind that I am not religious in any way, shape, or form but I have become passionately spiritual and truly believe in prayer/meditation.

In my past I have attempted to meditate without success. I think that my lack of success was due to not having true faith in the process and in a higher power or energy. I believe that faith is an essential aspect to meditation. Faith in our own powerful soul and faith in something bigger than anything we logically know. I was simply meditating for no true purpose.

The first purpose of prayer is to ask our angels, spirit guides, and god for help with our daily ongoings. Now sometimes this means asking for help during a difficult time in one's life. A second reason could be help with a task or something that we wish to accomplish or gain. Finally, it could be to ask help or assistance for someone else. Our angels have been with us since the day we were born and will continue to be with us until we die. Our spirit guides may be deceased family members or friends that have already crossed over to the spiritual realm. The final one is god. I personally don't identify with the term god as much as I do with the term Source. From here on out, I will be using this term. This is definitely a personal preference. Everyone identifies with different terms. Please feel free to choose your own. The second purpose for prayer is to give us hope and confidence that we do have "helpers" that are always with us even if we can't physically see them. They steer us in the correct direction which benefits in our earthly progress. If we aren't paying attention to the direction they are pointing us in, then we will continue to struggle.

Paying attention to their signs takes practice for sure. I will discuss signs in a later chapter.

I was always very anti-prayer due to the opinion that it seemed greedy and selfish. I didn't like the idea of praying because we needed something. Also, because it was typically attached to religion. I have abandoned that school of thought as I now believe that we have angels and others who are there to help us if we just ask for their help. They truly want us to ask for their help. I have firsthand had my prayers answered. Some naysayers may state that these were all coincidental. I truly do not believe that. I think as human beings, we sometimes chalk an amazing occurrence up to a simple coincidence. That is our brain and ego stepping in and saying, "that miracle could not have actually been a miracle." So let's look at a list of factual occurrences that have happened that in my opinion are true miracles.

1. Conception and the human developmental process
2. The Earth and it's amazing natural environment for all life to exist
3. Our heart beating with no outside help
4. Our brain having unlimited space to attain knowledge

Now those are just a few examples. If we were told that there was another planet in the universe that was as perfect and as accommodating as Earth, we would dismiss it and say that was impossible even though we live upon a perfect planet. My point being, is that we take miracles for granted every day because we see and live them on a daily basis. We are born into them so to us they aren't miracles at all but to an outsider, they would be. So how do we, as a species, begin to view our daily life as a miracle and believe that prayer will help our world as a whole? First of all, we each need to decide what the term "prayer" means. To me, I do not like prayer attached to the term "worship." This tends to adopt a level system in which we are simply at the bottom. I prefer to think of prayer as an earnest hope and appreciation for all that we have. Secondly, I think a lot of people are turned off by the term "prayer" as it tends to lean towards religious ideals. I know just hearing the word turned me off for sure. Maybe we should use the term "meditation" instead. Although that word may turn away some people who view it as hippyish or even crazy. Possibly we need a new term that bridges the gap or maybe each of us should come up with our own word that is comforting to us. I propose that task to you as you continue reading.

When you go to bed at night and wake in the morning how do you feel? Do you have feelings of stress, anxiety, nervousness, or even fear of what is awaiting you? A good majority of us feel some or all of these things every day and we live this way our entire lives. That is a very, very sad way to go through life. We don't have to live that way any longer. We can accept the help that our helpers on the other side are waiting to give to us. We can go to sleep at night with positivity and hope and wake in the morning knowing great things will unfold for us.

We live our lives in fear. The fear of disappointing ourselves and others. We have fear of failure and the fear of not living up to society's unreasonable expectations. Probably the biggest fear for most human beings is the unknowingness of death. So many people choose to ignore death and pretend as though it won't happen to them. This, as we all know, isn't the case. It will eventually greet all of us, with what I believe, is a warm and loving embrace. All of our earthly worries and stresses will be washed away and all that will remain is pure bliss. More on that subject later in the book.

This fear can harm us in so many ways. In the next chapter we will dissect our feelings of fear and learn to dismiss them from our lives.

Fear and Our Earthly Classroom

The word fear is both a noun and a verb. As a noun, it is an unpleasant emotion caused by the belief that someone or something is dangerous. Fear is definitely an unpleasant way to live. The feeling of fear turns an individual's life into pure survival mode. As a verb, it means to be afraid. Why are we so afraid? We aren't born afraid. It is a learned way of thinking. We are taught from a very young age to be afraid and sometimes for good reason. Being fearful of a hot stove burner or a busy street are lessons that we should be taught when we are children. On the other hand, we shouldn't be taught to fear god or society. It is my thought that one reason that religion was created was to control the masses. When people are taught from an early age that if they do not serve god or attend church or do not live their lives by the words of the Bible or other religious doctrines, then there will be hell fire and shame awaiting them. Why would god agree with that? The Source (my term for god) that I believe in is all loving and would never want humans to be taught those lessons of fear and negativity. Source loves us unconditionally and only wants us to do our very best each day, love each other, and to learn from our mistakes.

The earth is our classroom that we attend each and every day. In this amazing learning environment, we learn how to act, how to treat others, how to love, and how to create. I bet you haven't thought about our planet, daily lives, and interactions like a classroom before. When we think of ourselves as life-long students, we probably wouldn't be quite so hard on ourselves and on others. It's one thing to want to do your best, but profoundly another to expect instant perfection from ourselves. When we enter any level of schooling do we expect to know everything that we will be taught? The answer is absolutely, no. Afterall, we do not come into this life all-knowing.

We are humans who are in no way perfect and make a lot of mistakes. The only way to learn and to grow is to make mistakes. If we were born perfect and flawless then what would be the point of this life adventure that we are all on? Perfection, in my opinion, is boring and very mundane. The best aspects of an individual, and in fact anything, are the imperfections. Try to think of something or someone that is perfect. That is a pretty daunting task if you ask me. Flaws, in a sense, are pure perfection because individuality is so important to our soul's growth. Even though we are all connected and all come from and return to the same place, we need to be our own creative entity because creativity is fuel for our soul.

I want to share this Buddhist story to put the idea of perfection into perspective.

A Buddhist priest was in charge of the garden within the famous Zen temple. He had been given the job because he loved the flowers, shrubs, and trees. Next to the temple there was another, smaller temple where there lived a very old Zen master. One day, when the priest was expecting some special guests, he took extra care in tending to the garden. He pulled the weeds, trimmed the shrubs, combed the moss, and spent a long time meticulously raking up and carefully arranging all the dry autumn leaves. As he worked, the old master watched him with interest from across the wall that separated the temples.

When he had finished, the priest stood back to admire his work. "Isn't it beautiful," he called out to the old master. "Yes," replied the old man, "but there is something missing. Help me over this wall and I'll put it right for you."

After hesitating, the priest lifted the old fellow over and set him down. Slowly, the master walked to the tree near the center of the garden, grabbed it by the trunk, and shook it. Leaves showered down all over the garden. "There, that is better," said the old man, "you can put me back now."

Nature and the universe, in which we reside, is far more miraculous than any organized creation we could come up with. To think that we can disrupt the natural course of nature for the sake of tidiness is clearly wrong. Our planet itself is so remarkable. From the depths of our oceans to an example like that of the jungles of the Amazon, astonishing life exists and thrives. These environments are what I like to think of as, "fine-tuned chaos." They are the most beautiful oxymoron. Now that is just our planet. The universe, as an infinite whole, is a mind boggling beauty. It spans total infancy with miraculous stars, black holes, planets, and I'm sure so many things that we have yet to discover. What is more beautiful than infinite light, blackness, and energy? It is a canvas of intricate detail and wonder. Just stare up at the sky on a clear night and the amazement will fill your soul with wonder and happiness.

So back to this idea of fear. We should never make decisions based out of fear. Also, we should really try not to let fear motivate us. Now, can at times, fear motivate us to accomplish things? Things like completing a college degree or filing our taxes on time. The answer is yes but it still is not healthy for our soul. Fear equals disconnection and emptiness. To fill the emptiness, we create expectations. Sometimes these expectations come true but more often, they do not. I think it's safe to say that we all despise the feeling of fear, yet most of us live within its grips every day. I would assume that fear stems back to the first humans that were on earth. Around every corner of their daily survivalist lives lurked danger. They were literally in survival mode one hundred percent of their existence. They were fearful of being attacked by predators, of starvation, and concerned about protecting their families. From the beginning of our existence, this planet, although amazing, poses fear upon us.

How do we begin to relinquish fear and live without it? Well, the answer is more simplistic than you may think. First of all, we have to tell ourselves on a daily basis that we will not live our lives in fear. Whenever I begin to get a feeling of fear, I immediately say to myself, "I will not live my life this way." Amazingly, this has really worked and has been very freeing. We just need to tell ourselves this at every instance when the thought of fear enters our psyche. Secondly, it's talking to our angels, guides, and Source on a daily basis. I do it throughout the day no matter what activity I am doing. My favorite way to communicate is during meditation. My meditation routine has three steps:

5. Get comfortable and close my eyes
6. Take three deep breaths. With the first breath, I think of the word, angels. With the second, I think the word, spirit guides and with the third I think the word, Source.
7. Begin asking for help in whatever way I need it

It's as simple as that. Just relax and allow your prayers to be heard. On a side note, keep in mind that prayers are always heard but they sometimes materialize in ways you might not think. So keep your eyes and ears open and pay attention. I promise you that after doing this, you will not allow fear to rule your life. You will begin to feel comfort and support. Now of course the thoughts of fear may return again but if you continue to do this, eventually it will subside so you can live the life that you were meant to live.

There are two basic motivating forces: fear and love. When we are afraid, we pull back from life. When we are in love, we open to all that life has to offer with passion, excitement, and acceptance. We need to learn to love ourselves first, in all our glory and our imperfections. If we cannot love ourselves, we cannot fully open to our ability to love others or our potential to create. Evolution and all hopes for a better world rest in the fearlessness and open-hearted vision of people who embrace life.

-John Lennon

Free Will

I ronically, free will is our savior and also can be our demise. Free will allows us to learn as humans but also creates greed and negativity. It has started wars, committed crimes, and even dropped nuclear weapons. On the flip side, it has built monuments, cured disease, and spread incredible love and hope.

When we are given choices and different directions in which to go in life, we are able to choose where we would like to go. Sometimes we choose correctly and often times we do not. Now you may ask, how can we know for sure that there is a definitive correct and incorrect path? I have asked this question over and over and arrived at this answer: our souls create a contract of sorts before our conception. This soul contract entails all of the lessons that we choose to learn in this particular life on earth. These lessons can range from forgiveness to empathy. This concept of our soul creating a path of lessons that we need to learn in our future incarnation may seem like a strange concept, but it is what our soul does. As our soul transcends from lifetime to lifetime, new lessons are to be learned. If we don't complete the lessons in our life, we will have to repeat them until they are learned.

So back to the question asked: How can we know for sure that there is a correct path? We know this because the information is locked in our soul vault. Our soul knows the genuine truth. Our genuine truth. The true test for us as students is to learn from the incorrect paths and not fall into a negative and repetitious life pattern. Believe me, I have been guilty of this throughout my forty-five years of life. Free will is an amazing gift that Source bestows onto each one of us. Without it, we could not progress intellectually or spiritually.

We come into our life with a purpose or a mission although, due to outside influences and other variables we can stray from these purposes. Our soul travels on a journey from life to life trying to learn the lessons that we need to learn. When people ask, "what is the meaning of life?", the answer is growth through learning. Lessons and learning are why we are here. Our soul begins its journey with a blank slate and with each new life we live, it builds and builds the knowledge that it needs to eventually rise to the level of enlightenment. Our soul never dies. It lives on for eternity. Now, our physical body does die. It is simply (not that our extremely complex and miraculous body is simple) a shell or container that houses our soul and allows us to live upon this planet. Our body ages and grows tired but our soul only grows in wisdom. Do not fear the physical death. In actuality, it isn't a death at all. It is simply a transition to a different existence. A blissful and peaceful existence.

What is enlightenment? For this answer I will combine my interpretation with one of Matthieu Ricard, a Buddhist monk, photographer, author and humanitarian. He states that enlightenment is a state of perfect knowledge or wisdom, combined with infinite compassion. He goes on to say that enlightenment is an understanding of both the relative mode of existence (the way in which things appear to us) and the ultimate mode of existence (the true nature of these same appearances). I believe that true enlightenment comes when all of our life lessons are attained and our ego dissolves and is nonexistent. Our ego is created by our brain and society. Although we need a bit of ego to live and survive in our earthly life, it can get the best of us and lead to a negative way of life. It can cause us to seek out power and possessions that are truly not needed to progress our soul. All that our soul craves and needs is love, empathy, creativity, and compassion. These are the qualities which create an enlightened foundation of pure soulful perfection.

I will leave this chapter with a story of an ancient Taoist farmer.

There was once a farmer in ancient China who owned a horse and with it he farmed his fields. One day the horse got away and ran off. The farmer believed this to be terrible news and the end of his farming. What would he do without his horse? He would not be able to farm his fields any longer.

The next day, the horse returned with six other horses. The farmer stood in amazement. All of his despair was washed away in an instant. He would not only be able to farm his fields, he would be able to farm in a much more efficient and beneficial manner.

This is my analogy for reaching enlightenment through many lifetimes of learning. With each life we lead, we gain another horse to help to farm our fields. Finally, our crops have grown to perfection.

Infinity

Infinity is probably one of my favorite topics of discussion. It can be a concept that can be difficult for the human mind to wrap its head around. Are there things that continue endlessly forever and ever? Yes there are and they are difficult to dispute. Infinity is a beautiful thing. It is not beautiful because it allows us to not be fearful of death or an end. It is beautiful because its complexity is truth, yet it is simplistic at the same time. Is a circle infinite? It is because it never stops or starts. If you cut it, then it does have a definitive end and beginning but if it stays intact, it goes and goes. That is a very basic example of infinity. On the more complex end of the infinity spectrum is the universe. We can't view it in its entirety as we can a circle. For a moment, close your eyes and imagine yourself on a path throughout the universe. This path literally never ends. It extends in infinite directions for an infinite length. Can you see where it is taking you? Is it difficult for your mind to think about that?

Typically, the human mind needs definitive answers to questions and it needs a concrete beginning and end to everything. Infinity has none of those things.

Let us take a look at what I believe to be the four primary infinite concepts:

1. *The soul*
2. *Love*
3. *The universe*
4. *Numbers*

Now, each of these topics could be a book on its own but I will dissect them in a shorter fashion.

The Soul

The soul is a concept believed by some and dismissed by many. Different faiths and religions have their own feelings on the subject. For example, most sects of Christianity believe that the soul, upon death, will be judged by God and then determined whether it is worthy of going to Heaven or the feared alternative, Hell. To many Christians, God is to be feared. Conveniently, this can be used as an extremely powerful control tool. Of course humans want to go to the blissful Heaven for all of eternity and to accomplish this, we must follow the strict life rules brought forth by our religious elders. In my opinion, any faith basing its ideals in fear is not a healthy one.

Another western religion, Islam, takes the belief that, upon death, the soul separates from the body and then transfers from this world to the afterlife. An angel of death appears to the dying to then take their soul. The sinner's soul is extracted in the most painful way while the righteous are treated easily. Believing in and afterlife is one of the six articles of faith in Islam. The deceased are in an intermediary state, until the great resurrection. At the time of resurrection, it will be revealed whether they go to Heaven or Hell. Again, this is another faith that teaches fear-based beliefs.

Both Christians and Muslims do not believe in the idea of reincarnation. For them and pretty much all western religions, the soul does exist but only gets one shot at life. You better get it right the first time because there won't be a second. I have to say, I am not a big fan of the notion, "be perfect your first time around or suffer dearly."

Now let us switch to some eastern religious views of the soul. Hinduism takes the stance that a universal soul or God named Brahman takes on many forms of various gods or goddesses. Hindus believe that there is a piece of Brahman in everyone and this idea is referred to as the Atman. The Atman, or soul, are eternal, infinite, and indestructible. For Hindus, the individual soul is recognized as unique yet at the same time is simply an illusion. Also, Hinduism has the belief in reincarnation. A soul lives many lives until it has perfected itself and returns to Brahman. Contrasting to Hinduism, Buddhism does not believe in a soul or a creator God. Although they do refer to our energy being reborn, rather than using the term soul.

That is a very brief nutshell of a few beliefs of what the soul is. My thoughts on the subject of the soul are a bit different. Imagine a giant ocean of water. That ocean is Source and is pure love and energy. We as individuals, are a mere droplet of water or energy poured out of this massive ocean. Our soul is removed from Source and placed into our body which is born into human form. We live our lives as individuals so we can learn the lessons necessary for our progression. When our physical body dies, our soul is poured back into the great ocean of Source. We return to human form as many times as we would like for our soul to become complete. Some souls may complete their journey quicker than others.

When we do return to heavenly bliss between each lifetime, there is no god to judge us. We simply look back on our life with our own judgement. We have a life review where we can watch our life in movie form and we do not only relive our emotions throughout the review, we feel the emotions of the others that we came in contact with. Our soul then learns all perspectives of our actions, not just the perspective of our own self. This is an aspect that we sometimes have difficulty accomplishing when we are living within our own human ego and is a crucial aspect to the review and our progression.

Love

Love is something that we can all discuss and relate to. Every one of us, at some point in our lives, have felt true love. It could be with our parents, siblings, friends, children, or a spouse. Even though we all have felt love, would all of us say that it is infinite? Look at it this way, love is a transferable feeling in that it moves from person to person and generation to generation. Love is the most important thing in the universe. It is the best way to discipline because gentleness inspires respect. Love never dies even when our physical body expires. We continue to love the people who have passed onto the other side and their souls continue to have love for us. The argument that if you can't see, touch, taste, smell or hear (the five physical senses) something, then it's not real. You can't see love but is it real? Of course it is. Nobody can deny that. Feeling and seeing are two very different things.

Love can and does over-power pretty much anything in this world. It is the strongest and most powerful feeling that exists. Love is stronger than hate and more powerful than fear. It never dies and never ceases to exist. It is truly infinite. Now love can definitely be damaged and thrown away. I'm sure many of us have experienced that. Sometimes we do not treat love as we should. We often take it for granted and do not realize the validity of it until it is gone. This is one of those life lessons that we need to learn to not repeat.

Also, I would like to add something additional pertaining to love. True love, in my opinion, is one-hundred percent vulnerability. You can't have true love without both people being completely vulnerable to one another. I only wanted to throw this in because I have personally experienced relationships where one person was totally vulnerable and the other person was not. This is definitely an aspect that can contribute to the demise of a relationship.

The Universe

I have a question to propose to all of you. When does the universe begin and where does it end? Take all the time you need. No matter how much time you take, it will never be enough. You or I will never be able to answer that question. Of course there are many theories on this but they never truly answer the question in full. The big bang theory, for example explains how the planets and our universe were created but what created that huge explosion and what created whatever created what created that. I have a secondary question: Does everything that exists, have to be created? That answer should come fairly quickly to you I would think. It is very difficult to argue that everything that currently exists and has existed in the past, was created. If everything has a creator, then there can never be a beginning or an end. What created the big bang? What created Source? What created the first microorganism that created Darwin's theory of evolution? Do you see where I'm going with this? The universe is an infinite rabbit hole that never began and will never end. I personally find comfort in this although I understand that many people do not. If there was an end to the universe, I would actually be disappointed. The thought of a large wall encompassing us. I relate it to the movie, The Truman show. The scene where Truman realizes his life amidst his town is a farce. He realizes the sky is a wall and his disappointment is shown.

We accept the reality of the world with which we are presented. It's as simple as that.
-Christof (played by Ed Harris in *The Truman Show*)

Numbers

Although numbers do not have the philosophical questions attached to them like the previous topics do, they are in fact infinite. Again, it is pretty impossible to argue that numbers are not infinite. Just as with the infinancy of love, we all have personal experience with numbers. Both love and numbers are factual and subjective. We can't see that numbers are infinite due to the fact that we could write and write for our entire lives starting with the number one but we would never finish. The fact that numbers go on forever is a fun and more basic way to look at the idea of infinity.

Clarity from Chaos

I am going to begin this chapter with a personal experience. A few years ago my marriage of close to ten years ended. Although there were many differences and obstacles involved with the relationship, a divorce was not the answer for me. Unfortunately, the split happened anyway. It turns out that some relationships have an expiration date and some candles cannot burn for a lifetime. This person was the love of my life but as we all know, that doesn't always save a relationship. Having children together made the situation even more difficult and painful. I found myself basically amidst an unwanted new beginning. A do-over that I didn't want to do. At the time it certainly didn't feel like a fresh start with endless hopes and possibilities. It was more like a dark and depressing downward spiral that I was having difficulty managing. Each day seemed more difficult than the previous. I was a lost soul that was attempting to "lean into the sharp points," a saying that I began to grow fond of.

One day I heard about a book written by Neil Peart, the drummer of the band Rush. It was titled, "Ghost Rider: Travels on the Healing Road." The subject of his book wasn't anything related to music. It was the very sad story about how he had lost his daughter and wife within a single year. This book became the beginning of my salvation. Although I would never think to compare what he went through to my divorce, his words became like a warm blanket for my pain. His struggle with darkness was almost incomprehensible and yet he managed to come out of it on the other side of the tunnel. This was amazing to me. It truly inspired me.

Some changes look negative on the surface, you will soon realize that space is being created in your life for something new to emerge.

-Eckhart Tolle

At that same time I began spending any free time I had at my local library. It became my home away from home and sanctuary. The inspiration that Neil's book gave me somehow led me to the spiritual section at the library. I literally can't remember when it actually happened but from that moment on, my entire world and belief system changed. I couldn't get my hands on enough books. The topics of near-death experiences, mediums, past life regressions, and spirituality consumed me. In my earlier years I had a passion for learning about religions and different types of philosophies but I never explored these subjects. I had found a passion upon this new horizon.

Now you may think that religious studies and spirituality would be one in the same but in actuality they could not be more opposite ideals. Religion, in my opinion, is created by human beings for many reasons while spirituality is your soul knowing the Source that it came from and will return to. It is much more of a true belief than that of religion. Religion creates rules and strictness to control the masses. Spirituality has no need for all of that because you feel it from within, not from the words uttered from pulpits. I am not saying that all religious beliefs and practices are wrong by any means but there are some teachings that I believe cause much more harm than good.

I have actually lost track of how many books I have read. It has been one after another after another after another. My kids always ask me, "how many books are you reading?" My answer is usually, "I'm not quite sure."

Around the same time, I was referred to a medium who was also a counselor. At that point in my life I needed the advice and insight that she offered me. I went to see her on a very cold and snowy day in February. It was an eye-opening experience that changed my life forever. She was able to look into my life in a way that I certainly hadn't been able to do. The spiritual sense that was bestowed into my soul that day was a major game-changer for me.

This fueled my interest in these topics even further. As I learned more and more, my mind opened more and more. I began meditating and practicing prayer on a daily basis. Every day I would do this and I began to slowly climb out of the hole I was in. I used to think that life was a pile of difficulty (I'll use that more polite word, difficulty, than the one I really thought) and stress sprinkled with moments of happiness. It was definitely a "glass is half empty" way of living. I no longer live my life thinking that way. It did take a long time but it was a journey that I am so incredibly thankful for. I don't know where I would be if this would not have happened to me. I learned that in the midst of chaos there is opportunity and that most great changes in life are preceded by chaos. I exited dark chaos and entered a new world of bright clarity.

At any point in your life have you found yourself in a depression or struggle? I'm sure you have. We all have at some point in our lives. I don't know that my path would work for you as well as it has for me but I would recommend that you give it a try. You never know, it could do wonders for your happiness and mental state. You really don't have anything to lose.

If you are skeptical, and I definitely was, about prayer ask yourself this: what can it hurt? If you are thinking that all of this sounds wishy-washy and ridiculous, then stop reading now. Close the book and go on with your life as you have been. But if there is even an inkling of curiosity that you are feeling deep down then go with that feeling. Go with your gut. Afterall, your gut is your soul knowing the truth. I learned this far too many times the hard way. We too often discard a gut feeling which many times leads to a poor choice. Remember: GUT = INSTINCT

I found many books that inspired me and changed my life. They changed my way of thinking and view on all aspects of life. One reason for writing this book was because out of all the books I have read, I never found one written from this perspective. I'm not a medium (although I would love to have that gift) and I have never had a near-death experience. I am just like you. A regular person with regular problems. I found faith within myself and within the spiritual universe which led me to true happiness. I believe that you can find this also.

"You must read, you must persevere, you must sit up nights, you must inquire, and exert the utmost power of your mind. If one way does not lead to the desired meaning, take another; if obstacles arise, then still another; until, if your strength holds out, you will find that clear which at first looked dark."

-Giovanni Boccaccio

Source

As I stated earlier, I prefer to use the term Source instead of the traditional term, God. It just resonates and makes more sense to me personally. The word Source by definition means a place, person, or thing from which something comes or can be obtained. The word god is defined as the creator and ruler of the universe and source of all moral authority; the supreme being. Ruler of the universe seems a bit tyrannical to me. Also, moral authority paints a picture of judgement that I feel is untrue. It is a subtle difference but I believe there is a difference.

This chapter is probably the trickiest for me to write due to the fact that out of all the subjects I am writing about, this is the one that we, as humans, know the least about. Well it is the least our brains know about. Our soul knows the subject very well but unfortunately, our minds tend to control our human existence.

For me, this is the pure irony of our lives. Since Source is where we come from, we have little, if no recollection of it. The joke, if you will, is that with each lifetime that we return to this planet, a veil is placed over our memories of where we have been in past lives and in-between lives. Even though this is frustrating, it is absolutely necessary for this to happen. Without the veil we wouldn't be capable of experiencing our current life and learn our necessary lessons. We would only think about what had occurred in our past and not focus upon our future. Focusing on the past, closes the door to new experiences. Also, if we didn't have this "memory erasing," we would long for the peaceful serenity of Source. The in-between bliss which we had left.

I believe that Source is pure energy and love. If we come from pure energy and love then by simple deduction, that is what each of us is. Sometimes that is difficult to see when you analyze human beings. I know that I used this analogy earlier but I'm going to again because I feel it makes the most sense. We are each like a droplet of water that is removed from a giant ocean of water. That ocean of water is Source. We are that body of water, we come from that body of water, and we return to that body of water. Another analogy that I love is that Source is a giant wintery cloud and we are each snowflakes. We begin as water, turn to snow, then back to water again. The infinite circle of life that our soul is upon. We are always energy even though we change form.

Near-Death experiences (when a person dies and is revived) are fascinating to me. Many people say that during a near death experience they come into contact with Source. They usually describe it as light, warmth, energy, or love. When they have this contact, almost all have the same feeling. They don't want to leave and they feel one hundred percent unconditional love. They also say that there is absolutely no judgement placed upon them. There is only acceptance. Can you blame them? Would you want to leave?

I have always had difficulty with the idea that we are shamed and judged after our lives have ended. To me, there is no sense or truth in this. How could we come from something that will eventually punish us? Doesn't the opposite make much more sense? We do not learn from being judged. We instead learn from judging ourselves and from the mistakes that we have made in our lifetime. This way we can reflect on our life and come to the realization that we did make mistakes or we did hurt others. We can then begin to learn and grow from these realizations.

Let's look at this from a more earthly point of view. When we are children and we do something wrong and our parents scold us, we don't do it again out of fear of being scolded again. On the other hand, if we reflect on a time in our life when we acted poorly or hurt someone and judge those actions ourselves, we realize we were wrong. We then learn and we grow from these experiences. Also, aren't we taught from a very young age (at least I hope most of us were) not to judge other people? However, a large majority of the world's population does judge and believes that their creator will be a judgmental tyrant who punishes us. I have never understood how humans could buy into this idea. It most likely stems back to fear and control. I considered making a chapter about how fear and control are connected but I will cover it throughout the chapters. People who are fearful of failure, acceptance, and death tend to grasp to try to control every aspect of their life. The interesting thing is that these individuals appear to be very strong and even sometimes powerful. It's ironic that this appearance is nothing but a facade. True strength and confidence originates from vulnerability and humility and does not rely on over- compensation.

Personally, I would not have an ounce of respect for a creator who was judgmental. Would you? Do you have reverence for people who judge you? Here's a question for you parents out there and this will end the chapter: you created your children, correct? Do you judge them harshly and with cruelty? Do you instill fear into them to control them? Do you threaten punishment if they want to choose their own path and not the one that you choose for them? Now if you do, I will try not to judge you but if you do, maybe rethink your judgement. It isn't helping anyone.

Powerful Stuff

It's interesting that I am tackling this subject in December amongst the prime holiday gift buying season. We as human beings tend to place great importance on material possessions for many different reasons. I know many people who use material things to fill a void in their life. Whenever I think of people who do this, my mind instantly goes to images of the tv show Hoarders. These people have usually had traumatic times in their lives that have led them to filling their painful experience with stuff. It is a very sad situation to witness. Obviously most people don't have such extreme issues with material items but it can still be unhealthy.

I have always considered myself to be somewhat of a minimalist and most people who know me would definitely agree. Stuff just has never really pleased me. I actually enjoy the challenge of living my life with little amounts of material possessions. I believe that these things that people view as rounding out or completing their lives are actually weighing them down and creating an incorrect focus. The saying "keeping up with the Jones" is what our society thrives on. Getting the newest iPhone or an expensive vehicle is what propels many people to what they think will create happiness in their lives. The truth is that none of this matters. None of this will make you happy. I have known so many individuals who appear to have everything but in actuality have nothing. They tend to be depressed because they are always looking to acquire the next big item. I will let you in on a little secret, the next big item that you purchase will not fill that empty void. It will however certainly become the last big item and hold little to no meaning in your life. The last item in a sad line of materialistic waste.

When each of our current lives end, what will you be thinking about in those last few moments? A car, your big house, name brand clothing, expensive purses, jewelry or will you be focused on something completely different? I will answer this with absolute certainty. You will have other things on your mind. You will be focused on love and breathing. Hopefully the people you love will be by your side. Maybe you will be able to reminisce about fond memories that you shared. I can remember soon before my grandfather passed, he sat with me and shared old photos from his life. You know what he didn't share with me? He didn't tell me how much money he had in his bank account or how many amazing houses he had lived in. It meant so much to me that he did this and I am certain that it meant so much to him, especially because he had never been sentimental before that. It seemed that he knew that soon it would be his time to go and he wanted the end to be special. Moments like that are the important and crucial things that each one of us needs to appreciate.

People, especially Americans, want more and more. More possessions, more power, more control. Why is this? Do those ideas make us happy? They sure do not make me happy. Sometimes it may appear so on the surface, but if we dig a little deeper, we may find that we couldn't be more wrong. It's very sad to say but it seems that Americans have developed a sense of entitlement that is quite a disgrace in my opinion. Our way of life is the best and takes precedence over the rest of the world. Many feel that their own life is more important than everyone else's. Nobody is above anyone else and no person's desires or needs outweigh anyone else's. Everyone is unique and different in their own way yet we are all one in the same as souls.

Let's discuss the concept of power. The ability to influence others and their behavior with your words, ideas, and actions is how power is accomplished. People have sought after power since the beginning of existence and I'm sure they will until the end of existence. Positive things can be accomplished with power but many negative events have occurred throughout history because of it also. Having a hunger for power usually results in harmful results. This can be seen throughout history. There is a long list of dictators and leaders that have shown this to be true. Hitler, Mussolini, and Genghis Khan are prime examples of this type of negative power.

Whereas, having a humanitarian cause that leads to power usually has positive results. People who have a true and positive cause and who believe in the good of society as a whole will always be triumphant. A great example of this would Mother Teresa. She was the patron saint of missionaries and also a world-renowned teacher. After some time, she left the missionary and stated that she had a spiritual calling to leave the convent and help the poor while living among them. Her efforts gained attention from the world. She never sought out this attention for her noble acts but it ascended upon her.

-Mother Teresa

I think we can find a link or common place between the need for power and the need for material possessions. Both are filling a void. A void that is a bottomless pit of sorrow. Just as that "stuff" won't be with you on your deathbed, neither will the power. And if you believe that your powerful legacy will be appreciated for future studies, unless that power did the world good, it will not be appreciated. It will be studied and learned from its wrongfulness. Morality and love will be remembered and appreciated.

That which you create in beauty and goodness and truth lives on for all time to come. Don't spend your life accumulating material objects that will only turn to dust and ashes.

-Denis Waitley

Ordinary riches can be stolen, real riches cannot. In your soul are infinitely precious things that cannot be taken from you.

-Oscar Wilde

Empathy

When you see another person struggling, what do you feel? Do you turn and go on your way or do you stop and try to help? Do you instinctively feel what they are feeling? Empathy is a quality that I think could save all humanity. To have the ability to understand the feelings of others is an amazing thing. The old saying of "putting yourself in the other person's shoes," has always stuck with me. Whenever I am in a situation with someone else, I always try to feel what they are feeling and think what they are thinking. It seems to come naturally without any effort. I am, by no means, patting myself on the back. I am just being honest. By doing this, you enable yourself to see all perspectives of a situation. This is beneficial in so many ways to you and to the other person. It allows you to step outside of your own head, ego, and perspective. If everyone could do this, the world would be a much happier and more peaceful place.

Empathizing and sympathizing are two different things. Empathy means to experience someone else's feelings. It requires an emotional component that not all humans possess. To truly feel what that individual is feeling requires a love from within. A love that only wishes the best for others. On the other hand, sympathy means to understand the other person's suffering. It is much more cognitive in nature. Sympathy is compassion that keeps its distance. Empathy is compassion that has no distance.

Empathy also has an element of selflessness. We get so caught up in our day to day ongoings that sometimes we forget that other people have problems too. When we are empathetic towards someone in need, we can begin to help them heal. The best therapists are those that have empathy. Being a therapist with no empathy is like being a sun with no warmth or an ocean with no water. I believe that deep down, we are all empaths. If we would just take the time to tune into the feelings of others, we could access this helpful ability. Although, before we can do this we must become in tune with our own true feelings. Being in tune with our own pain and suffering and how those feelings influence our daily life, is crucial when we attempt to console others. Instead of burying our feelings or setting them aside, we should embrace them. Afterall, we cannot run from ourselves. When we attempt to try, we end up right back where we started. It would be like running a marathon but finding out that we went the wrong way and had to start over again. Also, we will never grow and progress if we do not first confront our own feelings. If we learn to confront our feelings, good and bad, we will then find a way to tune into others' feelings. The path to aiding others is to first aid ourselves.

Once we begin to mend our own emotional ailments we can do great acts for humanity. Is any intimate relationship possible without empathy? It is absolutely not. If we cannot deeply understand and feel our partner's, friend's, or spouse's feelings then the relationship will not succeed. Another aspect of empathy proving positive in relationships is when we are able to realize that we are acting badly and can realize the pain that we are causing to the other person. If we cannot see that we are causing pain to another, every relationship that we attempt will ultimately fail. We will jump from relationship to relationship and most likely end up alone or in a very volatile situation. We will never have a deep and meaningful relationship with anyone.

True empaths love to help people. They live to help people. I don't know if I would refer to myself as a true empath but I truly look forward to helping people through their times of struggle. I'm not sure why this is but it has always been how I have felt. I love to listen and offer whatever help that I can. Why are some people empathetic and others are not? That is an excellent question. Maybe it's due to their upbringing. There could have been a lack of love and compassion for those individuals who lack empathy or there could have been excess of love for those who possess empathy. Are we born with empathy or is it a learned behavior? I believe that we are born empathetic, loving, and creative. So basically I believe that we are born pure. It's all of the outside factors throughout our lives that turn that infant purity into something else.

If we all do attain empathy at our core at the beginning then we can seek out to reinstall it. I often wonder if there are people who have no desire to be empathetic or is it that they are just incapable of doing so. I believe it is the latter. It seems to me that they are damaged souls that need empathetic repair. Maybe a good exercise for those of us who do possess empathy is to seek out those who do not and attempt to offer them kind words and repair. This sounds like a daunting task while at the same time a very rewarding one. To help another soul could be the greatest thing we ever do in our lives and instilling empathetic restoration in another would prove itself to be beyond beneficial.

Could a greater miracle take place than for us to look through each other's eyes for an instant?
-Henry David Thoreau

When we honestly ask ourselves which person in our lives means the most to us, we often find that it is those who, instead of giving advice, solutions, or cures, have chosen rather to share our pain and touch our wounds with a warm and tender hand. The friend who can be silent with us in a moment of despair and confusion, who can stay with us in an hour of grief and bereavement, who can tolerate not knowing, not curing, not healing and face with us the reality of our powerlessness, that is a friend who cares.
-Henri Nouwen

Art and Creativity

Every human at its soul is love and creativity. These qualities make up our core foundation. Without either of these things, we are nothing and life would be meaningless. We want to love and be loved. Deep down, our soul craves a oneness with others. This oneness equates to love. As a species, we search out newness which is creativity. Every invention, artistic piece, and new idea is due to our deep desire to create. Even if you aren't an artist by definition, we are all artists. We all seek to create in some fashion. I'm sure you have had ideas and thoughts that have never been thought of before. You may not have acted on these ideas but never the less they did come from you. Instinctively, this is how our soul operates.

When I was a kid in elementary school, my favorite day of the week was Thursday. That was the day that we had art class every week. Even though I wasn't necessarily great at visual arts, I loved them. It gave me a feeling of true happiness even if the finished product wasn't visually amazing. Any form of art always intrigued me. It was a way to be free from the restraints of the otherwise regimented aspects of life. I think most kids embrace this feeling. As some people exit out of childhood, they lose this desire to create. This is a fundamental flaw of many people. Many parents convey to their children the idea that once we exit childhood, we must leave behind our soul's need and craving for creation. To lose the desire to create is very damaging. It can cause us to get lost in the downfalls of society and materialism. If we all could stay connected with our inner artistic child, we would benefit greatly.

To me, creativity is so amazing. Whether you create with paint, words, or a guitar, it is freeing and completely fulfilling. I found my creativity was rooted in words and music. When I was eight years old I stumbled onto my older brother's drums and never looked back. Playing drums and creating music was my passion for the majority of my life. When I was in high school I discovered writing. Words and the way they could be put together was fascinating to me. Sentence structure, storytelling, and placing my beliefs, thoughts, and opinions into words became a second passion for me.

What do you think our soul craves? Does it yearn for a cubicle or the hopes of a big office? Does it seek out financial success? Does our soul hope to work at a mundane job for our whole life? The answer is absolutely, one-hundred percent, no. Our soul is meant to create and enhance the world. We, as human beings, have so much unlimited art to contribute to this world. All we have to do is tap into what our individual self has to offer and go with it. Once we do that, the world and our soul will only benefit.

Creation equals growth. Without new ideas, growth can never happen. Civilization has always relied on human creativity to prosper. If you look at each and every civilization, you can view what they brought to the world in regards to ingenuity. Whether we are looking at Archaic, Greek, Roman, or current times, the creativity is constantly visible. Progression of human existence is the greatest art expression there ever was and will ever will be. Invention, of any type, has two purposes: need and creativity. We create for practical necessities as well as expressive necessity.

Art has existed since the beginning of time. Even before we had advanced tools or vocal communication as we do today, humans had the desire to create. Scientists have discovered drawings done by very early humans that date to seventy-three thousand years ago. They are rock paintings depicting human and wildlife scenes. At this point in human evolution, we were basic hunters and gatherers but we still had an artistic soul. Those early humans were most likely not taught artistic expression, they simply did it because of an inner need to create. I'm sure it filled their soul with happiness. To be a fly on that cave wall and witness these drawings being created would have been an amazing sight.

Do you think there has ever been a human that didn't have any type of desire to create? I bet that would be a difficult thing to find in the history of humans. Yes, some people are definitely more inclined to a creative lifestyle than others but we are all creative in our own unique way. Some people may be creative in coming up with new business models while others may innovate with culinary skills. There are musical artists, literary artists, cinematic artists, and architectural artists to name just a few. If you think about it, almost every aspect of our lives can be viewed as artistic. Simply going for a stroll can be an art. Our perspective and view of the world is artistic in itself and the real creative thing about the human psyche is that we each view everything differently. That is true art. Art is one-hundred percent perspective. I have always told my children that art is never wrong. There are no rules when it comes to artistic expression. When they were very young and learning to color, I would tell them to stay in the lines. The moment they could do this, I then said to never stay within the lines again.

Can you imagine what children would do without art? I think they would be lost little souls with little happiness in their lives. If no human had ever created any type of art as a child, what would they be like as adults? They would be a flat and mundane version of themself. They would not understand what expressionism is or what happiness is. What would the world be like? It would be sad, colorless, and somewhat like that of a black and white photograph from the eighteen hundreds where the people never had smiles on their faces. We wouldn't have much of a world at all. It would be nothing but extreme blah. I would have no desire to live in that type of world.

I strongly urge you to encourage all types of artistic expression in your household not only for your children but also for yourself. No matter what it may look like, do it. Just start creating. I bet once you begin doing this, you won't be able to stop.

Consciousness

What is consciousness? It is total awareness of yourself and the world around you. We each have our own unique consciousness. This is our soul's accumulation of lessons learned, individual personality traits, and our own creativity.

There is a strong argument that consciousness is simply our mind and that when our mind no longer physically exists, our consciousness ceases existence also. I just cannot get on board with this argument. Our brains, in all of their amazement, are the most complex computer systems that have ever existed. They have unlimited storage space and a never-ending thirst for knowledge. The human brain has solved mathematical mysteries, designed structures of awe, and written great novels but there are some things that the brain cannot accomplish. The brain does not attain intuition or a "gut" feeling. When you have an instant feeling, good or bad, about a person or a situation, that is something other than your mind at work.

Secondly, the brain does not feel or give love. Love is something that is difficult to describe with the brain. It is almost ineffable. Our brain can distinguish, analyze, compute, describe, and learn practically anything, however it does not have the ability to love.

I believe that the brain and our consciousness co-mingle and assist one another while remaining separate entities. The brain is an organ that functions while living and does not function after physical death. Consciousness is not an organ of the body. It is alive before our physical existence and lives on after our physical existence. The way in which they work together is that our consciousness stores information and memories that are attained from our brain and from each of our lives on earth. With all of this extensive knowledge, our soul grows and progresses into perfection.

So, what is consciousness other than awareness of self and all that surrounds self? It is soul. Our soul is not our brain or our physicality. It is something so much greater than that. It is energy and love and purity. It is who and what we truly are at our foundational core. Our true self, or soul, isn't our appearance or the knowledge that is stored in our brain. It is our essence of loving oneness with each other and essentially everything in all of existence. It is our connectedness to Source and our knowing that is where we originate and to where we will return to.

As newborn babies, we enter this world with pure infant beauty. Our new brain has no knowledge within it. We haven't learned communication, right or wrong, or how to "be." Infant souls have agreed to come into another earthly life for their soul's growth. Although this is a difficult thing to do, we all do it over and over again. We know what our mission is but the hardest part is starting over as a human with no knowledge within our brain. Imagine having to conduct a surgical procedure without any medical knowledge. We would know that we were supposed to help this person on the operating table yet we couldn't. That is how our infant soul feels on a daily basis. Although difficult and challenging, our infant soul possesses pure love. This simply exists within us. This is something that does not have to be taught. It is a pure and intuitive connection between our soul and those around us. We all desire giving and receiving love. For some, it may be buried deep inside of them due to damage they have experienced throughout their life, but whatever the case the possession of love never dies within our soul.

If there is no presence of soul, how is this so? If we are only a brain, how can we love? A bodily organ cannot love. It can function in incredible ways to keep our body operating day to day. It can learn and solve problems. It can balance unlimited thought processes from its left and right lobes but it cannot love. Here is a prime example of how the brain is incapable of loving. Have you ever known someone that you had the desire to love for whatever reason? Maybe they were smart or funny or physically attractive. Your brain could recognize all of these positive traits but yet that "special thing" just wasn't there. That key element that is needed for us to fall in love. Although the recognition was there, your brain could not force you to be in love with that individual. If the mind was capable of love then that "special thing" would not be necessary. That "special thing" that is necessary for true love can only be found in one's soul or consciousness.

When two souls fall in love, there is nothing else but the yearning to be close to the other. The presence is felt through a held hand, a voice heard and the sight of a smile. Even though a simple touch. Souls do not have calendars or clocks, nor do they understand the notion of time or distance. They only know it feels right to be with one another. This is the reason why you miss someone so much when they are not around. Your soul feels their absence-it doesn't realize the separation is temporary.

-Lang Leav

Any soul that volunteers for the journey of reincarnation is courageous indeed. It is a journey of many steps, many difficult lives, many births and deaths - often traumatic. Yet those who are relatively new to the journey are still close to that cosmic urge to experience, learn and evolve. They have more enthusiasm for life than most of us.

-Barry

Control

One day my nine year old daughter randomly said, "I think it's better for someone to steer the boat than to control the boat." Talk about a real Zen statement. Many of us attempt to control our lives and frequently, the lives of others. Sometimes we will go to such great lengths to accomplish this that it can lead to unhappiness within us. We feel that if we cannot gain control, our lives will not live up to that of our expectations. If we could just steer our lives through our free will and not with our expectations, it would unfold naturally and with beautiful wonder.

Why do humans seek to control? I believe the answer is simple, yet sad: fear. This horrible feeling that always seems to haunt us. When we are scared of a certain outcome from a situation we attempt to control it. I have witnessed people go to extreme measures to control a situation. Whether it be by intimidating another person or shaming them, it is usually obvious why it is being done. Why do many followers of religious faiths do what they are told? They follow orders or doctrine so they will not be punished by the god they believe in. They love and devote their life to this god yet they fear greatly. This fear that is instilled in them is a very powerful control device.

The belief system that I have adopted has no fear and therefore it has no need for control. A life that has an absence of the control factor is miraculous. I feel that it is a very positive and freeing way to live one's life. Having faith should not equate to following orders. True faith should be felt from within by seeking out what resonates with each one of us. All people, no matter what they believe, come from and will return to the same place which is Source. While we are on this physical planet, hopefully all of us have a belief system that makes sense to us.

Another reason to seek out control could be due to trauma or abuse that occurred in one's life. Maybe there was a point where you had no choices because you were held under the restraints of another's abuse. As you get out from under this abusive control, you may take every measure possible to take control of your life and circumstances. In this case, you must overcome the control issues by facing and working through the abuse that you experienced.

Often, coinciding with abuse is abandonment issues. When an individual has been abandoned, they seek to control any relationship that presents itself. They may purposely sabotage relationships or prematurely end them in fear that the other person will leave them. If this behavior continues, the person will live their life in solitude until they confront this issue.

In this day and age it seems that a vast percentage of the population deals with anxiety issues. This feeling causes us to feel as though our life is spiraling out of control and we cannot do anything to stop it. Again, attempt for control steps in and takes over. To feel anxious is to feel weak. Human beings usually despise the feeling of weakness. When someone is giving off the appearance of extreme confidence, almost to the point of arrogance, more times than not they are experiencing anxiety in some form.

I spoke earlier of the expectations of perfection imposed on us by ourselves and from society. Perfectionism is a quality that many people strive for on a daily basis. They feel that if they aren't perfect, they are weak and frail in comparison to others although they may not appear so on their exterior. This is extremely harmful to their psyche. It can even cause mental and physical illness. Perfectionists are typically less happy and more stressed in general. They tend to beat themselves up and wallow in negative feelings when their expectations are not met. They often have trouble tolerating or coping with any type of chaos or disorder. Perfectionists typically do not possess the quality of acceptance. They struggle with maintaining coping skills that are necessary for having a healthy life.

Insecurity is yet one more human quality that can lead to having control issues. Self-doubt, social anxiety, and rejection can lead to insecurity. These can be very traumatic issues that cause pain. Pain = Insecurity = Needing Control. It is crucial to deal with the pain that resides within us. Once we do this, the equation changes to: Recognition = Acceptance = Letting Go.

Doesn't the second equation seem like a much healthier and happier way of living? Living in the first equation is the same as living in a prison. Free yourself from your own personal prison so you can begin to actually live your life and not be fearful of it. You can release the reins if you truly want to.

JUST LET GO!

When you see someone who needs power and control and will not stop until they get it, you are actually seeing someone who is deeply afraid of life. Fearful people can only have things their way.

-Me

Hope and Possibilities

Hope is one of the major aspects of life that keeps us getting out of bed every day. Without hope, what do we have? We would have an empty glass. Hope is the reason our glass should always be half full. We have all had moments of feeling hopeless for sure. Hopefully these feelings are fleeting. Even in the worst moments of my life, there has always been some thread of hope at my core. I am so very thankful for this.

I believe that hope and faith can be very similar but they do have some major differences. I will discuss these in detail in a later chapter. They are both something deep down that we can't force to happen. They simply exist within us. I love that each and every day when I wake, I have this feeling that something great could be following that beautiful sunrise. Every day is full of possibilities. These possibilities are endless and can come to us at any minute of every day. Sometimes these possibilities or opportunities are on a large scale and sometimes they are on a smaller scale Sometimes they knock us completely off our tracks but sometimes we may pass them by if our eyes and minds are not completely open. I have known pessimistic people who, when confronted with an amazing opportunity, thoughtlessly dismiss it. Their glass is so empty that amazement passes them by on a daily basis. These people don't possess a true faith within their soul. They may be religious (I've had firsthand experience with these individuals) but they aren't faithful or hopeful.

Praying should be full of faith and hope. This should equate to happiness in one's life. When I sit down and pray, I am instantly filled with happiness. This isn't due to the fact that I think I am pleasing an intimidating god. It is due to the fact that I am truly believing that there is hope surrounding me at all times. This is a very powerful feeling. Hope has kept people alive in horrific situations throughout time. Hope has kept destitute societies from perishing. Hope could be one of the most powerful concepts within our existence. If you are a hopeful person, hold onto it tight and do not let go If you lack hope, open up your soul and believe in its truth. If you let it in, you will prosper in all of its possibilities. It will free you beyond all measure.

Something that I have always taught my kids is to relish in the feeling of anticipation. Anticipation is a type of hope. It is hoping that a future situation or event will be a positive one. Anticipation has always thrilled and excited me. It is one of the great gifts of life. When we have hope for something, attached to that is the anticipation of that thing fostering. Learning to enjoy the process of possibilities, hope, and anticipation is an amazing human trifecta. When you were a child, what was more exciting, Christmas Eve or Christmas Day? The eve of an exciting event is always more exhilarating than the actual event. Every day is an incredible eve of your life. Anticipation, Anticipation, Anticipation. It is to be savored and reveled in.

Do you feel that each day is an opportunity for you to enrich your life? If you don't, let's figure out how you can change that. Ask yourself, why do I lack hope and dwell in a dismal mindset? Getting to the bottom of this question is the first step. Be honest with yourself when answering the question. What is lacking in your life or influencing you so strongly to be so pessimistic? Is it something from your childhood or possibly something more recent? Do some hard soul-searching to figure out the answer to this. Your happiness definitely depends on it.

Once you figure out where it stems from then you can begin to tell yourself that whatever it was does not have control any longer. Repeat over and over to yourself, "I will not live my life this way any longer. I will move forward in a positive way each and every day. Also, you can begin to say your prayer and ask for support from your helpers to aid you in this daily task. With your new strong will and this help, I have no doubt that you will succeed in your new journey of hope and possibilities. Always remember to focus on the open doors that life presents and not the closed ones. Typically, the journey of our life is the true point, not the destination.

Life is what happens when you're busy making other plans.

-Allen Saunders

I will leave you with a short story that I am fond of that demonstrates hope very well.

Do you have your umbrella?

As a drought continued for what seemed like an eternity, a small community of farmers was in a quandary as to what to do. Rain was important to keep their crops healthy and sustain the townspeople's way of life. As the problem became more acute, the townspeople decided to gather one evening to pray for rain.

Many people arrived at the meeting and the farmer that was leading the meeting greeted everyone one by one. As he walked to the front to begin the meeting he noticed that most people were chatting across the aisles and socializing with each other.

When he reached the front his thoughts were on speaking to the attendees and starting the meeting.

His eyes scanned the crowd as he asked for silence. He noticed an eleven year-old girl sitting quietly in the front row. Her face was beaming with excitement.

Next to her, open and ready for use, was a colorful and extremely large umbrella, much bigger than her in fact.

The little girl's beauty and innocence made the man smile as he realized how much faith and hope the girl possessed. No one else in the group had brought an umbrella with them.

All came to pray for rain but the young girl had come expecting an answer.

This story demonstrates true and absolute hope. Why did the little girl have an elevated level of hope that the adults did not? Why do many of us lose hope as we grow older? Maybe we need to try a little harder to think positive and make the decision to live a life that is half full. Afterall, the first step to getting anywhere is deciding you are no longer willing to stay where you are now.

Hope is a waking dream.

-Aristotle

Our Purpose and Place

A client of mine asked the question, "what am I supposed to be doing with my life? What does it all mean? What is my purpose?" My response was, "where you are is where you are supposed to be." I know that is a simple answer and to skeptics, it sounds like an easy cop-out but it truly isn't. Life is a series of stepping stones that lead to our greater good. Without the first step there could not be the last. Have you ever sat back and recalled the series of events in your life that led you to where you are now? Some of these memories may be positive and some may be negative but they are all of extreme importance.

Coincidence is said to be a remarkable concurrence of events or circumstances without apparent connection. This is somewhat of a contradiction in my opinion. The most remarkable things in life don't happen by pure chance or luck. Also, all events are connected. Every moment of our lives is connected to the previous and to the next. This simply a fact of life.

Earlier in chapter one I listed a few factual miracles that exist. We can look at this same list in regards to coincidence. The first, being conception and the human developmental process. What do you think the odds are of human beings, or any complex life form, being created out of pure chance? In order for any of us to exist, many unlikely events had to happen in precisely the right sequence. The exact sperm and egg cell sequence of your DNA code that makes you the unique individual that you are is a one in two-hundred-fifty million chance. That is just one "coincidence" that had to occur. Not only did this need to happen to create you, it had to happen over and over again for thousands and thousands of generations from the beginning of existence. That is one incredibly, astonishing, and amazing coincidence!

The latter part of the first example is how we develop from one stage of our life to the next. Conception is amazing in its own right but developmental progression is quite another. What if we were to stay in infant form for our entire life? Well we would not continue to exist. The first infants ever born would have died soon after and there would not have been future humans. Infants are clearly incapable of lone survival. I have a spin-off question that I don't believe any of us can answer unless you are quoting a religious scripture: if those first infants needed guidance and protection, who provided those things? Kind of a "what came first, the chicken or the egg" question. This is one question that I think will be answered during each of our returns to Source. I definitely do not possess the know-all or arrogance to even begin to answer that question.

The second of my examples was the Earth and its suitable and natural environment for all life to exist. Let us examine the Big Bang theory which is the leading theory of how our universe came to be. It states that the universe expanded from its initial size due to high density and high temperature. After this initial expansion, the universe cooled to allow subatomic particles and atoms to form. Giant clouds of elements which included hydrogen, helium, and lithium began to form. This later created gravity, stars, and galaxies. So, if this theory is correct and it very well may be, what was before the Big Bang and what was before whatever was before that? Also, what are the odds that this sequence of events led exactly to you and I? Again, this would be a remarkable coincidence.

The third of my examples was our heart beating with no outside help. I have researched this and I know the medical reason for how this occurs, which is as follows: the heartbeat is triggered by electrical impulses that travel down from a small bundle of specialized cells called the SA node. When I was reading all about the ins and outs of the heart, it made my example even more miraculous and non-coincidental than I had initially thought. The whole sequence of events that have to take place for our heart to beat once is incredible but for it to continue these events for a lifetime is beyond comprehension. For this to have been mere chance, in my mind, is impossible.

My final example was our brain having unlimited space to attain knowledge. The brain not only controls almost all functions of our body but it is more amazing than the most sophisticated computer on the planet. I have been reading recently about brain grooves. The human brain has many grooves that are physically visible. Brain researchers have revealed that when a certain thought is repeated, positive or negative, often enough it forms a new groove. Future thoughts automatically return to the familiar groove. Over time, these grooves deepen and it takes greater effort to change those thought patterns. This is fascinating to me. Something so abstract and with no physical presence as a thought can transpose itself into a physicality. If we can feed out brains with positive thought, imagine how our brain could change for the better.

How could the human brain come to be by mere chance? That's like saying that the highest functioning computer just appeared one day and was not created. If I travelled to the moon and came back with a computer that I said I found on the surface but I also somehow knew that nothing or no one had created it, would anyone believe that? Of course not. Believing that something so sophisticated transpired from an explosion is very difficult to subscribe to.

Basically, I am saying that everything we are and everything that has happened throughout existence is not simply luck. It is so much more. It is bigger and more astonishing than we could ever comprehend. To deduce it all to mere luck is lazy in my opinion. Our lives, whether we can recognize it presently or not, is exquisite and angelic chaos.

One of my favorite quotes is from legendary guitarist Joe Walsh:

You know, there is a philosopher who said, "as you live your life, it appears to be anarchy and chaos with random events and non-related events smashing into each other and causing this situation and that situation, and then, this happens and it's overwhelming and it just looks like what in the world is going on? And later when you look back at it, it looks like a finely crafted novel. But at the time, it don't."

-Joe Walsh

Our purpose, as I stated earlier, is to learn and grow our soul to its fullest potential. Even, if at moments, it doesn't seem like you are learning lessons and life isn't working out the way you would like, believe me it is your own finely crafted novel. Also remember that lessons stem from struggle and challenge, not from ease and comfort.

Our Own Unique Settlement

No human being should ever settle no matter what the situation is. We should however settle into our own happiness. For so much of my life, I wasn't able to settle into happiness. I was always trying to settle into someone else's happiness. Trying to please another is nothing but a pitfall of disparity. So often, many people let go of their own happiness to concede to make someone else happy. It is one thing to compromise, yet it is quite another to lose yourself for another.

A great aspect of our soul developing and finding its true path is to be true to yourself. If you are finding yourself in a relationship where you aren't fulfilling your soul's creative destiny, then I believe you should take a step back and reevaluate your circumstances. Are you happy in this relationship or do you feel smothered by misery and unhappiness? Are you getting the fulfillment that your soul desires? Are you being your true self or are you putting on a facade to please your partner? For me, the answer was unanimously, No. I cannot tell you how many times I have found myself in this type of situation. This is a horrible place to find yourself in.

A true soulmate or true love would never stifle their partner's creative force. They would support it fully. If this support does not exist within the relationship, could it be viewed as a waste of your soul's time? I believe so and if this pattern is repeated throughout your life then it is a waste of an entire earthly life. If we are repeating negativity then we are definitely not learning or living, we are merely existing. We were not intended to exist. We are meant to thrive.

We have all heard the words within self-help information that states: "work on making yourself happy and healthy before you attempt a relationship." Of course this makes logical sense but do many people go through the self work that is necessary for this to happen? I would bet the answer is no. I know I never did until recently and I have gone through a lot of pain and struggle to get where I'm at. I was always happy being me but now I am truly happy and proud of me, and I feel fulfilled. I can wake up each day knowing that I can be me. I can create the things that resonate with my soul. I'm not happy because I'm in a relationship. That always seemed to be a major aspect of my definition as a human. Now, I am in a much different and healthier place in my life. I can finally breathe a sigh of happiness. I have let the real me, or soul me, be present and thrive. It is so amazingly freeing.

Codependency can be detrimental in so many ways. Whether it lies within substance abuse, obsession, or a relationship, it can dominate our lives in a negative manner. Relationship codependency is dangerous territory. Many of us have found ourselves in this situation. Some, more extreme than others, but regardless, they aren't healthy. Even people who are of the mindset that they have to be involved in a relationship or think that they have to be married to be fulfilled are codependent upon a relationship. They feel that this defines them as an individual which could not be more incorrect. Our soul is the true definition of who we are. Our creativity, love, and presence defines who we are. We will never have healthy and happy relationships until we know and love who we are.

Once we know who we are, we can begin to figure out where we want to go. Do you know who you are and where you want to go? I know that is a difficult question for a lot of people and can take some time to answer. First, ask yourself what makes you happy? What can you create that will fill your soul?

The things that have filled my soul are as follows: (I am listing them chronologically, not by importance). The first was writing and performing musically. Second, it was having children. Lastly, it is what you are reading right now. Music, children, and writing fills my soul. I recommend that you think on it for a while and then make your own list. Trust me, once it comes to you, you will never be the same again. Once your soul is filled with what makes you happy, the world opens up for you to create and fill in your blank canvas.

Look around you and look inside you. How many people do you think are settling? I will tell you; a hell of a lot of people. People are settling everyday into okay relationships and okay jobs and an okay life. And do you know why? Because okay is comfortable. Okay pays the bills and gives a warm bed at night and allows one to go out with coworkers on a Friday evening to enjoy happy hour. But do you know what okay is not? Okay isn't thrilling, it isn't passion, it isn't the reason you get up every day and it isn't life-changing or unforgettable. Okay is not the reason you

go to bed late and wake up early. Okay is not the reason you risk absolutely everything you've got just for the smallest chance that something absolutely amazing could happen.
-Purple Buddha Project

The Island

This chapter is purely hypothetical, yet extremely important. Let's imagine a person was born on a desert island alone. There is no mother or father or anyone else. Like I said, hypothetical. This infant was able to survive and have no harm done upon it. This person experiences all of the phases of growth and becomes an adult. Throughout growth, there is no outside influence other than nature. What would this human believe? Would there be any spiritual element to this individual? I'm wondering if the only focus would be on survival. I believe that when survival became more or less a routine, this individual would seek out more. The "more" would be faith or belief in the unknown "something."

For the sake of making this hypothetical story more of a story, let's give this individual a name. Bob sat in thought among the endless island hours, his brain began to wonder how he got there and why he was there. Was he the only one of his type to exist? He had no concept of conception or civilization. He didn't even understand much about his physical body except for its daily functions. This had to cause him quite a great deal of confusion. He was a mystery to himself.

Bob learned by trial and error and from the mistakes that he had made. He would slowly display progress in hunting and gathering, tool making, and other survival tasks. He would grow older by the day, but without societal influence, would he mature? Would he remain at the maturity level of a child or infant for that matter.

My main question would be, did he feel a connection to anything? He most likely would to his physical surroundings: the island itself, the ocean, the animals. This connection would be more out of necessity and survival. Would he ask himself, is there something more out there? Is there something bigger than me? I am sure these are thoughts that early humans had. The only difference here is that Bob was alone. Trying to evaluate what a lone individual, with no exposure to another human, would believe is something that I would love to know.

Let's take this one step further. Say that Bob lived out his life alone on the island and one day he died. He would return to Source as we all do between lives. After his soul was ready to return to earth for another go of it, would he progress and mature at a quicker rate? Even though he returned to a solitary life on the island, would he feel more of a soulful connection to Source? How many solitary lifetimes would it take? Just some food for thought.

Can you even begin to imagine being a mystery to yourself? No one to explain your past or heritage. No one to teach you anything. You would be a sole soul. Trying to imagine life with absolutely no influence is like trying to picture infinity. Purity in its most basic sense, that is how we should attempt to live our lives. It is such an abstract concept. It is incomprehensible, yet pure and beautiful at the same time.

If we could somehow harness this basic purity of our soul and its creative purpose and have it coincide with societal existence, we could begin to have a truly spiritual planet. One-hundred percent acceptance of one another with empathetic compassion is necessary to accomplish this. This may seem like an impossibility, and it very well may be, but it is worth an effort.

I have a proposition to all of you out there. For the next day or two, whenever you encounter anyone, whether you know them or not, do not view them as a race, gender, by name, by age, or any other typical way of viewing someone. Think of them as a glowing soul of energy. They all look exactly the same when you do this. I try to do this on a daily basis and it really is amazing. You begin to realize that we all do come from the same place and we all want the same basic things. I have found that when you do this, all of our human judgement goes out the window. It opens us up to accept and care about one another. Isn't this how it should be? Viewing people by how attractive they are, the clothing they choose to wear, how their voice sounds, or any other physical trait limits our acceptance of them.

No one likes feeling judged. Back off and let people live. We're all on some type of journey, all evolving and growing.

-Psychic Grace

Faith With No Walls

L ike I stated previously, I am not religious. When I say that, I do not mean any offense to any of you that are. I have respect for all religions and the people that are followers. Afterall, we all are headed to the same place. We may take different roads to get there, but all of our roads lead to bliss.

One of the issues that I have with organized religion is the view that you have to attend an organized gathering every week in a specified building. Apparently, that is where God (Source) is. Now, I do like the community aspect of gathering at church, however I do not care for the guilt aspect if you choose to not attend. Setting the community portion of church aside, why is it necessary? Prayer and faith is a very personal choice and aspect of life. I prefer to pray by myself because it is so personal. To me, it should not be a regimented practice. To sit for an hour and a half in an uncomfortable seat is not my idea of a soulful experience. It should be completely comfortable and relaxed. I pray and communicate with Source on a daily basis, not on a weekly one.

Where is Source? It's not here nor there. It's not up or down or right or left. Source is absolutely everywhere but the strongest place it is, is within all of us. When you wake up in the morning, there it is. Every minute of the day, there it is. Source is never "somewhere else." Your soul knows this and feels it constantly.

Some of the most moving prayers I have even heard and seen were from the cotton fields of the south during slavery. The songs that those people would sing while working in the blistering heat of those fields was so soothing and beautiful. It was prayer for them. They were treated so horrifically, yet they were able to unify their voices to form a musical prayer. They didn't need a building to congregate in. They felt everything they needed for prayer within each of their souls. They could have been anywhere and their souls would have felt the touch of Source. True faith is located wherever we are and in any activity that we are participating in.

Since prayer is such a personal thing, create your own. I told you how I prayed earlier and if you want to try my way, feel free. Maybe mine doesn't sound like it will work for you. I think that's great. Take the time to create your own.

Since creativity is crucial to our soul's development, by creating your own prayer, your soul will be doing backflips of happiness. I feel that if we each create our own prayer, it will have so much more meaning than if we simply had it read to us from a book.

Again, I am not trying to discourage religious people. I am attempting to have everyone find their own path that they can walk upon to their own happiness and fulfillment.

The minority, the ruling class at present, has the schools and press, usually the church as well, under its thumb. This enables it to organize and sway the emotions of the masses and make its tool of them.

-Albert Einstein

Pain

Pain is inevitable and pain is necessary. Pain brings us to our knees and it also lifts us to the heavens. It makes us feel distant and connected. Since we will all experience pain at some point in our lives, how do we use it as a learning tool to advance our soul? We definitely learn from difficult situations and pain is always difficult whether it is physical or psychological. Pain shows us the dark side of life and teaches us to appreciate the upside of life. Imagine if we never experienced an ounce of pain throughout our lives. Life would be nothing but ease. Basically, we would learn absolutely nothing. Pain is challenge and challenge is what defines us and allows us to grow. Let's challenge ourselves to accept the pain and to work through it so we can definitively improve.

As humans, we cause pain and we take it on. What are some painful experiences of your life? I have had many. I know that I have caused many people pain and pain has been inflicted upon me. One of the most impactful and painful experiences we will ever experience is the death of someone close to us. This is the ultimate test of pain. I have lost many people during my life. Each loss had a significant, yet different effect on my life. How do we move forward after losing someone so close to us? We have to first, grieve. Acknowledge the person's life and death. Next, sit with the love that you feel for them and appreciate it for its beauty. Finally, realize that they have only left you physically and they are with you always. Relish in the fact that you will be with them again when you leave your earthly life.

I love to learn. I would prefer to learn by choice and on my terms but I have realized that sometimes life forces lessons upon us even though we may not have chosen it. These can be some of the most impactful lessons of our life. There are many painful learning experiences that are forced on us. Failure, divorce, a broken heart, mistakes, and depression are a few lessons that can be horribly gratifying, yet amazing growth experiences. How can we grow from situations such as these? From my personal experience, I learned to value being humbled and losing my ego. I learned to see situations from different perspectives and a very important thing that pain teaches us is patience. It is hard to grieve quickly. Many of us attempt to rush this process, but in the long run it will only delay the end result, which is acceptance and closure. It is a process that takes time.

We can become encompassed from only our point of view. This can be a terrible place to view the world. Imagine looking at a sunrise while laying on your back. It may be an okay view but it's definitely not the best one. When we only see from our point of view, we become emotional dictators attempting to control the relationship. Seeing life and relationships from many angles, creates more positive outcomes.

Our instinct is to run from pain and to avoid it by any means necessary. This is definitely an enormous mistake. I don't think we can appreciate true happiness unless we have gone through pain and struggle. It's like trying to appreciate a sunset without a sunrise. It's the balance that is necessary to achieve happiness. Life is a balance sheet of emotional turmoil and ecstatic bliss battling for control.

People are afraid of themselves, of their own reality; their feelings most of all. People talk about how great love is, but that's bullshit. Love hurts. Feelings are disturbing. People are taught that pain is evil and dangerous. How can they deal with love if they're afraid to feel? Pain is meant to wake us up. People try to hide their pain. But they're wrong. Pain is something to carry, like a radio. You feel your strength in the experience of pain. It's all in how you carry it. That's what matters. Pain is a feeling. Your feelings are a part of you. Your own reality. If you feel ashamed of them, and hide them, you're letting society destroy your reality. You should stand up for your right to feel pain.

-Jim Morrison

Without pain, without sacrifice, we would have nothing.

-Tyler Durden (played by Brad Pitt in *Fight Club*)

Appreciation

*Appreciation is a wonderful thing. It makes what is
excellent in others belong to us as well.*
Voltaire

What do you have appreciation for? My hope is that you have it for literally everything that surrounds us and that is us. From our planet to our love, from our endless creative possibilities to the functions of our mind, we should all have appreciation.

I think that far too many of us take our existence for granted. This can be easy to do if we cannot view life from outside of our own perspective. Sometimes in life, we only see what we choose to see and also from the viewpoint of our mind. What we choose to see isn't always what is the truth. The truth can sometimes be a difficult one to see. The sooner we can have this realization, the better off we will be.

One of the greatest gifts that we have is the ability to choose and carve out our own path in life. Our free will allows for this to be a possibility. Every day we wake up to choices that lead to possibilities. Do you ever think about that? Many people view these choices as more of a stressful to-do list than a daily chance of opportunities. The trials and stresses of daily life can sometimes over shadow this gift.

When we appreciate, we have a full understanding of a situation. In 2017 Forbes magazine wrote an article about appreciation. They listed ten benefits of appreciation. They are as follows:

8. **Your mindset changes.** When you change your mindset to look for the good instead of the bad in someone or a situation , you begin to notice just how fantastic they are.

9. **Your mood improves.** Psychologists have long said how our mood and daily outlooks change when we focus on positive things rather than negative.

10. **You engage at a higher level.** A recent study shows that when people give appreciation to others, their engagement score increases by 26%.

11. **Your ability to innovate improves.** Research shows that people who give appreciation to others experience a 33% increase in innovation.

12. **You build trust in relationships.** When we give appreciation to others, our relationships become stronger and more substantial.

13. **You will remain in a positive situation for a longer period of time.** When we are appreciated and show appreciation, we will want to stay longer.

14. **You increase your effectiveness.** Research shows that people who give appreciation experience a 22% increase in the results of a situation.

15. **You smile more… and apparently cry more.** There's something intrinsically nice, and good about appreciation that just screams, "it's the right thing to do." When people bring their heart and souls to a situation, there is an emotional impact on people. Appreciate, and you'll inspire some smiles and tears.

16. **You inspire greatness in others.** We all would love to be the person who inspires someone else. It turns out that it's not that hard to do when you give appreciation. Studies show that 88% of people who receive appreciation feel inspired to do great things.

17. **You create a story with a future.** Giving or receiving appreciation tells the other

person what you admire about them and their actions. When everyone is clear about this, that person is likely to continue with these positive actions.

I really like this list and how it shows that only positivity can come from appreciation. I think we just need to actively think about our appreciation for all aspects of life on a daily basis. Positivity affects so many things including: our health (especially stress, anxiety, and depression), our creativity, our motivation, and the overall state of the world. When others see you being positive, it's very difficult for them to continue a negative attitude. Positivity is quite infectious. We can all spread it like wildfire if we choose to do so.

Here is a beautiful story for you all. It was written by Nick Ortner for The Tapping Solution website.

A blind boy sat on the steps of a building with a hat by his feet. He held up a sign which read, "I am blind, please help."

There were only a few coins in the hat- spare change from folks as they hurried past.

A man was walking by. He took a few coins from his pocket and dropped them into the hat. He then took the sign, turned it around, and wrote some words. Then he put the sign back in the boy's hand so that everyone who walked by would see the new words.

Soon the hat began to fill up. A lot more people were giving money to the blind boy.

That afternoon, the man who had changed the sign returned to see how things were. The boy recognized his footsteps and asked, "were you the one who changed my sign this morning? What did you write."

The man said, "I only wrote the truth. I said what you said but in a different way."

I wrote, "Today is a beautiful day, but I cannot see it."

Both signs spoke the truth. But the first sign simply said the boy was blind, while the second sign conveyed to everyone walking by how grateful they should be to see.

In the future, when you sink into negative thoughts and lack appreciation, think back to this story. I know that when I first read it, it really struck a chord with me and made me feel very appreciative.

Ego and Selfishness

Navigating through life is not always an easy task. Our ego is something that is necessary for earthly life. It allows us to identify as our own unique "self." It also allows us to view the external world through perception. It is the part of us that evaluates, remembers, and is responsive to and acts in the surrounding physical and social world. The ego provides consistency to our daily lives by offering our own point of view. Thought and judgement are also a crucial part of the ego.

Even though our ego is essential for our survival, it can also cause us problems. Our ego sometimes can lead us in a superficial or judgmental direction. When we go down these unhealthy paths, we fall into patterns of unhappiness and non-contentment. We may temporarily feel fulfilled by these superficial ways but in the long run we will feel inner depression and unhappiness.

Since our ego filters everything that surrounds us through our own perception, it does not always positively guide us. Our ego has been taught that as humans we are imperfect, which we are, but this societal teaching forces us to compare ourselves to others. It forces unhealthy competition between us. Our ego causes depression, anxiety, and unhealthy and unrealistic expectations of ourselves. An ego-driven life is always striving for more; more money, more physical beauty, more material possessions. Our main importance and purpose becomes how we are viewed by others and not who we truly are as a human soul. This then motivates our actions through fear and insecurity. This type of motivation is harmful and meaningless.

Typically, individuals who live their lives in this manner do not connect to their true self. They aren't spiritual and creative beings. They may be religious, but seldom are spiritual. They have difficulty relaxing into a calm state of being. Imagine attempting to meditate when you are this type of person. I don't imagine these people would even attempt this let alone be successful at it.

Do you honestly believe that our soul cares what people think about the car we drive or how much square footage our home is? If this is meaningless to our true self, shouldn't it be meaningless to our ego? Our soul does care how much love people give to us and to others and how much love we give in return. It cares about creating masterpieces and working with others to create them also. We, as a species, need to do some serious soul searching. We need to deeply explore who we are at our core. We need to expel the notions that society places upon us. We need to focus on the things that make us soulfully happy. When we discover what these things are, we can participate in life in an egolessness manner. Activities like meditation and any type of artistic expression lead to this way of life. When we partake in these types of things, we are living in the moment. We aren't striving for more, comparing our life to that of another, or plotting to get somewhere that we aren't. We are just being. Have you ever been doing something that makes you so happy that you lose track of everything including time, thought, and motive. They all cease to exist in these incredible moments. In this moment your soul is vibrating at such a high level, your mind shuts off and true happiness is allowed to flow within you. Your soul is guiding the way and not your mind. This is what happens on a regular basis for artists and spiritualists. Sounds like an amazing way to live life, doesn't it? All you have to do is make the decision and have the courage to live your life in this way and you will be on your way.

We can never completely discard our ego. Like I said, it is necessary for our survival on this planet. What we can begin to explore and work on is recognizing when our ego needs to be put in check. We need to develop ego awareness. For instance, when our ego is being used for survival, that is a positive ego action. However, when we are judging others based on a superficial basis, this is a negative ego action. Learning to catch ourselves when these things occur is crucial for our development. Once you start doing this, it will become natural and eventually the negative actions or thoughts will be very minimal. This is similar to the practice of viewing people as souls and not as their physicality.

Selfishness ties in nicely with ego. People who lead ego-centric lives, are truly selfish and numb to others' feelings. They are only motivated by things and ideas that serve them. Also, they usually lack any sense of empathy. The ego or "I" can be very selfish. Selfishness can destroy relationships due to the fact that the individual is incapable of being an "us" and not an "I." We all have found ourselves in some type of relationship where the other person acted in this way. These relationships are volatile and do not typically last long. If they do continue on, it can be very harmful to the non-selfish person. It is almost a type of abuse. We need to be able to recognize selfish individuals and steer clear of relationships with them if possible.

Dear Self,

You have to stop being available to unavailable people. Stop giving so much of yourself to people who cannot even identify who they are. Self doesn't give anything to anyone who can't reciprocate. If these people do not sacrifice for you then they should gain nothing from you. Things of value require sacrifice. If people are too hurt, too busy, or just too damn stupid to see that you're the blessing they've been asking for, just fall back... Know your worth.

-Anonymous

Dreams

Dreaming is the best preparation for dying because in dreams we travel the same roads, out of the body, that we will take after death, when we no longer have physical bodies.

-Robert Moss

Dreams are the link between our soul and the other side. When we are in a dream state or REM sleep we have the ability to receive messages from our angels, spirit guides, and if we are truly fortunate, Source. Think of our mind as an antenna that is capable of broadcasting and relaying messages from the other side to our soul. Our brain is like a movie projector. It allows us to have access to amazing dream images that we would otherwise not be able to see. Have you ever had a dream about a deceased loved one? You awake with an extremely loving and happy feeling. It felt like you were with them again. Well, you were. Their soul made a visit to your soul. They wanted or needed to communicate something to you. Maybe they just wanted to let you know that they weren't gone from your life. The message was to convey that they were always with you even though they were physically gone. On the other hand, they may have needed to pass on some important information that they thought could help you or someone else. Either way, this is an amazing experience for you to soak in and take seriously. Unfortunately, so many people dismiss these dreams as pure fiction when in actuality they couldn't be more real.

The dream state can be similar to deep meditation. The actual closest similarity to deep meditation is that moment between being awake and being asleep. I'm sure you have experienced that unique in-limbo state of awake/sleep time when you lie down, close your eyes, and feel extreme relaxation. You aren't awake but not quite asleep. You enter a dream state different from the REM state dreaming. We can receive messages in both states but I wanted to identify the difference between the two.

One of the major differences between a dream message sent from the other side and a dream that isn't a message, is that the message dreams are almost always remembered. It is true that we can, sometimes, remember dreams that are not a true message, however almost all dreams that are true messages are remembered. Have you ever had one of these? I bet you have. I know that I have had a few. We need to be open-minded and willing to recognize these dreams when they occur. Do not brush them off as fictional coincidence.

One way we can remember our dreams and actually keep track of them is to have a journal or notebook next to your bed. The second you wake, write down everything that you can recall from your dreams. If we wait even a few minutes to do this, they can disappear from our mind. I know that I have had many instances where I wish I had written my dreams down. Not only could these dream messages contain important information, they can be fun to reflect on. Imagine if you could look back on your dreams from different times in your life. I think we all would enjoy that.

There are times when we receive a message through a dream that may not be from a deceased loved one or from someone that we have ever met. It is possible that we can be used as a conduit to communicate a message from the other side to someone in the physical world. You may ask, why would this happen? Well, a soul on the other side may need to get a message to a loved one but they may know that the individual would not be open-minded enough to receive such a message. This is the reason that they may need to find someone who can relay the message for them.

This is a dream that I had within the last year that has really stuck with me. I was actually able to convey the message to the people that it was intended for which was very important to them as well as myself. A simple dream was not simple at all. It was something that created healing.

A client of mine had lost her sister-in-law about five weeks earlier. I had never met her before so initially the dream caught me off guard.

In my dream, a woman whom I didn't recognize although I somehow knew who she was came to me and simply said, "please tell her I'm ok. Please tell her that I'm at peace finally."

It just happened to be that I would be seeing my client that next week. In the days leading up to our appointment, I went back and forth on whether I should tell her about the dream or not. I wondered if it would upset her or that she would think I was crazy and not believe any of it. After much consideration, I decided to tell her.

The day of our appointment, I found myself giddy with the excitement of telling her of my dream. Immediately after telling her, I could see it meant a lot to her. She told me that she would pass on the message to the woman's children who were having much struggle with their mother's passing.

I felt as though I had been chosen as a conduit for the situation. I truly believe that the message was real and I know that the message helped in the healing process for the family. Everyone involved in the situation was very grateful for the message.

Signs

We've established that a couple of ways communication occurs is through dreams and meditation. Another way is with the use of signs. There are all types of signs, that if you are paying attention, can signal that a soul, angel, or Source is trying to communicate something to you. Just remember that your mind has to be open to receiving them. Also, you have to really pay attention. When we are distracted by our life or stressed, we don't always notice these things.

The other day I was driving to work and pulled off into a parking lot to make a phone call. I looked up and saw a truck right in front of me. Written in huge letters across the side of it was the word Source. A few minutes later, I was stopped at an intersection and directly in front of me was a building. Written across it was also the word, Source. I was in awe. You can say that this was pure coincidence but that was too much "coincidence" to happen within a few minutes.

Another way that messages are sent to us are through music. I have a few songs that I have designated as songs that have meaning to me and I know when I hear them, a message of some sort is being sent to me. One of these songs was one of my dad's favorites. Whenever it comes on the radio, I know he's with me. I always get a huge smile on my face when it comes on. Do you have any certain songs that have strong meaning to you or that maybe you shared with a loved one that has passed on? Give it some thought and then pay attention when you are listening to the radio. When these songs come on, maybe someone is by your side.

Do you ever see certain number combinations on a regular basis? Sequences of numbers can definitely equate to a spiritual message. This happens to me many times daily. I am constantly seeing 111 or 222. These types of sequences can have strong angelic forces behind them and are a simple way for the other side to let us know they are with us.

You may be skeptical of these signs and I completely get it. The funny thing is this; the more we become in touch with the fact that we are more than just a physical entity and that we are a soul with depth beyond comprehension, all of these signs begin to appear to us. They speak to us and make sense.

Two lyrics from a couple of my sign songs:

I'm gonna free fall out into nothin
Gonna leave this world for a while

-Tom Petty

Says she talks to angels
They call her out by her name
Oh yeah, she talks to angels
Says they call her out by her name

-The Black Crowes

Our Life Pre Review

Some people who have experienced near death experiences have recalled having a life review. The life review is something we all experience when we pass over. Many religions believe that when we pass on, we stand before god and are judged on the life that we led. This is a religious fallacy. Source does not have any judgement regarding any soul. We are the ones that judge our lives. Doesn't this make a lot more sense? Like I said earlier, when we are judged by another, we don't learn. We just obey which is based out of fear and not love. When we view for ourselves, we learn. When we learn, we begin to grow.

This is what I propose; let's stop for a bit and take a heartfelt look at our life up to this point. Let's take a mid-life review of how we have lived. How have we behaved? What have we chosen to be the important priorities in our life? Did we treat our life and the lives of others with respect and graciousness? Waiting until this life is over to evaluate how we have treated ourselves and others is something we can avoid. For so many of us, we live our daily lives without much reflection. Human beings tend to focus on the future and not on the present. Our "plans" can hinder the way in which we live. Always looking for what's next doesn't allow us to look at what is right in front of our face. We can, in a sense, have a fresh start on how we live. The life pre review could change things for us.

We do make mistakes and that's ok. If we didn't, we wouldn't be human beings. The important thing is that we acknowledge and learn from our mistakes. We shouldn't be hindered or embarrassed by them. Have you ever learned anything without failing at that lesson the first time? Of course not. We fail at first, but then we succeed. Keep failing so you can be successful. There isn't a person in the history of mankind that hasn't made mistakes and failed at many things. Why are we so hard on ourselves when we make a mistake? The next time you make a mistake, instead of getting upset about it, appreciate it. Give yourself a break and accept your mistakes and take time to reflect on them. This will humble you and make you better. Any person who is successful at anything, has been humbled. Afterall, isn't that the point?

Humility and humbleness create amazing souls. We shouldn't view these qualities as unworthiness by any means. They are more of character-building qualities that should be regarded in a sacred manner. Humility is a very healthy thing even though most people would disagree. Here are six attributes of healthy humility:

18.   They acknowledge they don't have it all together.
19.   They know the difference between self-confidence and pride.
20.   They seek to add value to others.
21.   They take responsibility for their actions.
22.   They understand the shadow side of success.
23.   They are filled with gratitude for what they have.

How many of these can you honestly say apply to your life? Hopefully, they all do but if not, that's okay. Keep working at it and you will get there.

Go and make interesting mistakes, make amazing mistakes, make glorious and fantastic mistakes. Break the rules. Leave the world more interesting for your being here. Make. Good. Art.

-Neil Gaiman

The most valuable thing you can make is a mistake- you can't learn anything from being perfect.

-Adam Osborne

A life spent making mistakes is not only more honorable, but more useful than a life spent doing nothing.

-George Bernard Shaw

Acceptance

Acceptance can be one of the most difficult things we do in our lives. When we choose to accept, whether it be an idea, a person, or an outcome of a particular situation, we are making a commitment to welcome this with an open mind and heart. As human beings, acceptance doesn't always come naturally or easy. Our strong will and beliefs can often interfere with the process. Also, the way in which we were raised can really sway us to not be accepting. Try to set these things aside and look at a situation objectively. There have been many situations when I logically want to accept something but strong feelings have made it a challenge. Sometimes I really have to step outside of my own head and tell myself to accept. It can be similar to talking to a child. Children are not always accepting. Many times they just react, just as adults can. The difference is, adults should be mature enough to not be simply, reactive. Adults should use filters before reacting. Filters give us time to think and weigh a situation. I do know many adults who do not take advantage of this as I am sure you do too. So the next time you are in a situation and you are having difficulty accepting something, sit your inner child down and have a little talk with them.

One type of acceptance is forgiveness. This can be something that can heal our soul but it is easier said than done. Have you ever held a grudge against someone and found it difficult to forgive? I have seen this destroy families and friendships. It can be due to very small things sometimes, but for whatever reason the person cannot get past it. Our soul has no issue with forgiveness. It is nothing but pure love which easily forgives. It's our ego or "self" that has the problem forgiving. Our ego has been influenced by an array of ideas that are hard to break. We sometimes have to deprogram our minds to accept and forgive. This isn't an easy thing to do and many people never attempt to do so. I think that at some point in our childhood, we should have to take an acceptance and forgiveness class in school. If it could be ingrained in us as children maybe as we age it could come easier.

Love and acceptance seem to go hand in hand. Having unconditional love for everyone isn't always attainable but I believe acceptance can be. To accept is to be open-minded. To be open-minded is to be unbiased and unprejudiced. We have to let go of our preconceived bias. Bias can only harm our soul. Whenever we think in a biased fashion, we are treating ideas and situations unfairly. We need to teach ourselves to be objective in situations. What is the simplest route to viewing a situation objectively? I believe that being empathetic and trying to view from numerous perspectives is the key. Wouldn't you appreciate someone trying to see from your perspective? Of course you would. I think everyone would.

When we begin to practice acceptance, it can be a challenge at times, but it gets easier and easier to do and a domino effect begins to occur. The key is to make a conscious effort each and every day to make this happen. Acceptance is a state of mind. We choose our states of mindedness. If you tell yourself that you will be accepting of people and ideas, well then you will. How different would the world be if everyone told themself that every day? That is a world I would love to live in.

Here is a list published by Classpass.com of four ways to practice acceptance on a daily basis:

Nix Judgement

Try to avoid thinking of situations as good or bad and simply see them for what they are. There are things outside of our control that often create an outcome that directly affects us. It's normal to feel completely responsible in these cases and to harshly criticize ourselves for it. But this is rarely the case, and negativity is not the ideal path toward advancement. Sometimes we just need to do a little adapting.

Acknowledge Always

To be clear, accepting yourself doesn't imply weakness or mean giving up and staying in the same place. Practicing acceptance means respecting the process and your current place, and also acknowledging that everything is or can be temporary. Thinking of a situation in terms of the way it makes you feel helps to visualize an experience as such. For example, instead of thinking you're a failure for not getting a promotion, you thought you had in the bag, understand that this is just a feeling of disappointment that you are experiencing at the moment, and use it to revise your plan for the future.

Start With Self

Nobody gets very far by being hard on themselves, especially when the criticism is unwarranted. A positive mind pushes you forward, and when you acknowledge that you're capable of doing better, any shortcoming begins to matter less. Realize also that there are things you can let go of, things that don't serve you or your current situation. Approach setbacks in a positive way and embrace how they make you feel. You'll notice the feelings start to change as your understanding of the situation evolves. You might even learn a thing or two and prepare yourself better for the next time.

Find The Good

Some situations seem to be missing the light at the end of the tunnel. We've all been there. Even though it may seem impossible, there is always something to be happy about. It will take some time and effort, but developing the skill to seek out the positive is well within everyone's ability. The best tool to help you fully accept yourself is the ability to always find a way to be happy and move forward.

Setting goals for our future can be a great thing to do and it can help us to move in a forward direction. The only negative aspect to this is if we fail or the goal simply doesn't materialize. This can cause us to become distraught and sometimes depressed. We can plan but always keep in mind that if the goal doesn't happen, that's ok. Just let it go.

Remember that when things don't go according to plan, they go according to truth. No matter how painful the reality, it is reality nonetheless. There is dignity in facing the truth without trying to cut it down to a more manageable size. There is honor in acceptance.

-Vironika Tugaleva

Your Soul's Will

There may be times in everyone's life when we struggle and feel as though we are going nowhere. This is true for all human beings. Your soul is quite different however. Your soul will never cease to thrive. Your soul is infinite and therefore it's will is also. Infinity of the will of the soul is an amazing truth we all need to recognize. Appreciate that your soul never stops progressing and never stops existing. Believe that your soul is your true essence and that your physical existence is fleeting and temporary. Your soul came before your body and it will live on after you die.

What causes people to lack a belief in a soul? I think I have an answer for this. I believe that they have been hurt and struggle through life. They feel that since they have had a difficult life, how could there be something greater? How could the universe have dealt them such a terrible hand? This is where perspective comes into play. Instead of looking at their difficult life as a growth session for their soul, they think that life is meaningless. Many individuals become very jaded and resentful towards life as a whole. Life is pain and it is struggle. Once we can acknowledge this and use these things as tools to make us stronger, our lives will take on new meaning. Each one of us will feel a purpose for our lives. We learn so much from the pain and struggle that we experience. That's why we deal with it on a regular basis.

Our soul has a will that can never be destroyed. It has a level of spiritual strength that cannot be measured. The will of our soul continuously seeks knowledge, clarity, and creativity. It may take many lifetimes to fill our soul up to the top but eventually we will. Envision your soul as a cup, that with each incarnation, we add a little bit more. We add wisdom and knowing. We keep filling and filling our cup until we burst into enlightenment; The Big Bang soul burst.

We, as humans, have a will to live physically but this is no comparison to the will of our soul. Our soul doesn't have to worry about death like our physical will does. Most people worry about their death on a regular basis. It can become an unhealthy fixation for many people. On the other hand, there are individuals who suppress the thought of death. This is also very unhealthy and can stunt your growth. If we are focused on our physical death throughout our life, we cannot truly live and learn the lessons intended for us. However, since our soul has no fear of death, it never can be stunted in its growth. In a sense, the soul always gets a new beginning with each new incarnation. A clean slate of growth that adds up to a mountain of wisdom. That is a beautiful truth.

Our clean slate is like a brand new computer that is free from viruses and used up megabytes. It's a chalkboard on the first day of school. What do you want to write on your chalkboard? I want to write a masterpiece. I hope that you do too because I know that your soul wants to. Figure out what your masterpiece will be and once you do, start it and finish it. Allow your soul to be free with creativity. Afterall, this life doesn't choose you, you choose it.

Creative work is soul work and soul work is creative work. Every creative work in human history was created by the soul. It was not created simply by the mind. The mind conceptualizes the idea into a physical form. The mind can operate at many incredible levels but it can't create on its own. Art and creativity are pure and not analytical. The mind is of analytical persuasion while the soul is completely creative.

Art is purity and love is purity. Both are the substance of the human soul. Think about this, when you are in love and when you create art, doesn't one feel exactly as gratifying as the other? Sit and think for a minute about that. The feeling of the two is one in the same. Creativity, just as love, is a spark that happens within us. It's exciting and it brings great joy.

When it is working, you completely go into another place, you're tapping into things that are totally universal, completely beyond your ego and your own self. That is what it's all about.

-Keith Haring

Hope vs Faith

Hope and faith definitely have some similar commonalities but they are very different. Faith is a complete trust and knowing while hope is an expectation or desire for a certain outcome. The part of us that has hope lies within our brain and the part where faith is found is in the depths of our soul. The soul is the all-knowing abyss of faith that fuels us from one incarnation to the next.

Faith, in my opinion, is where we all seek to reside. We may not consciously realize it, but underneath everything we all do. For a decent portion of my life, I lacked true faith. I had points of getting close to it but never quite got there until recently. Even in the times when I literally had none, deep down I did long for it. It's kind of like enjoying solitude but there is part of you that has a deep desire to find another to spend your days with. Faith is the most wonderful companion that we can find. It is inspiring to the millionth degree. With it, there is nothing that you cannot achieve.

So where does belief fall amongst faith and hope? Belief is more of an acceptance of an idea. Our brain believes just as it hopes. Some people tell themselves that they believe in a certain ideology. Do they whole-heartedly believe what they have been taught or are they fearful to stray from the teachings. This can be seen quite frequently in children. When children are brought up to believe specific religious ideas or any idea for that matter, they usually stick by that teaching. Many unhealthy teachings such as racism, sexism, and general stereotyping can be learned at a young age. An installation of any belief system can cause our soul an incapability for true faith. The way that our soul breathes is by learning and deciding for itself what it has faith in. When the soul has faith, it resonates on an extremely high level which leads to genuine happiness and a feeling of contentment.

It is very important for children to have access to all different types of teachings and belief systems. Notice that I said access. This is much different than forcing a belief upon them. What does forcing accomplish? It only accomplishes confidence for the one forcing the lesson. It also releases fear for the one doing the teaching. Parents can be fearful that their children will stray from the religious lessons that will lead them to being "good" people. Possibly another fearful worry that parents have is that if the child doesn't believe, they will be cast into a dark hell-like eternity. It is understandable that no parent would want this outcome for their child. However, the reason that this type of thinking is a waste of time is because it simply is not true. There does not exist a hell-like eternity. It is nothing but a human-created farce. I wish that the religious world would abandon this teaching for the sake of humanity.

Stifling a soul is like smothering a brightly burning flame. Instead of smothering it, try fanning it. Fan the creative force that leads to having faith. Being told that we have a soul won't make you have faith in a soul. Learning about the soul and then choosing the lesson because it resonates deep inside of you is what it's all about. Never believe something because you are told to do so. Always question and always seek out answers. I hope and encourage that all of you read books about all types of beliefs so you can make your own choice.

To one who has faith, no explanation is necessary. To the one without faith, no explanation is possible.
                                        -Thomas Aquinas

Faith is an oasis in the heart which will never be reached by the caravan of thinking.
-Khalil Gibran

You have to grow from the inside out. None can teach you, none can make you spiritual. There is no other teacher but your own soul.
-Swami Vivekananda

Faith sees the invisible, believes the unbelievable, and receives the impossible.
-Corrie Ten Boom

Live, Live, Live

All of our earthly experiences and memories add to our soul journey. Have you ever heard the phrase, "making memories?" I truly love that saying and I know I've said it many times. It is a great mindset to have in my opinion. Life is not just hours in a day and days in a year. It is meaningful moments, one after another. We each can have a large role in creating memories for ourselves and for others. Remember the chapter about empathy? It comes into play here too. Help create unforgettable memories for people in your life. I always think to myself on a daily basis that we are making memories. Every moment with my kids, whether a stressful day or a relaxed one, is a day that we are logging memorable moments to our soul. This also takes conscious effort, but when you practice it, it is very rewarding.

Live your life with passion. Live it as if your soul depended on it (because it does). I have a few passions. Being a dad, writing, and playing music are the things that spark me. When you feel that spark on a regular basis, that is a passion. What is your passion? You may have one or you may have many. If you have many, consider yourself very lucky. These passions are so important. If it is a true passion, you will think about it daily. You may not be able to do it daily, but you do think about it. Sometimes with the daily life stresses we endure, it is difficult to make time for what we deeply desire. I can speak personally about this. Being a single dad with three kids and a full-time job, finding time to write can be a challenge at times. There are many moments during the day that all I think about is writing, but I can't. However, I know that it's a passion because this book is getting written. It flows out of me like a faucet that I cannot turn off. I bet you have a faucet too. Turn it on and let it flow.

When I was younger, before kids, marriage, and the responsibilities that eventually came, I felt that I did live my life to the fullest. In a sense, I did. I did the things that made me happy. I followed my passion for playing music which I have no regrets. I was a free spirit, in that, I had nothing tying me down. I was living as a typical twenty something year old. Now that I am older and somewhat wiser, I am realizing that I could have been doing so much more. I could have been starting my writing adventure at twenty instead of at forty-five (better late than never). Although without those extra years of life experience, the writing may have been lacking in substance. I suppose we all reflect on our lives in that way. Life substance can definitely add to creative output.

It could be said that with each year we live, we gain more depth. I hope this is true because depth equates to growth. Experience usually leads to maturity and growth which is soul fuel. Think of your soul as a baby that needs to constantly be fed and nurtured. It cannot evolve without the nurturing that we attain from the lessons from our earthly life. Every time we go through a difficult experience, we gain knowledge which then transfers to our soul. Our soul then compiles all of these lessons. This is soul growth.

Soul growth happens constantly from the day we are born. We are always learning lessons whether we choose to or not. Even though we are always learning, we need to take an active role in truly living and in feeding our soul. What is the definition of truly living and feeding our soul with what it needs to grow? Again, that is based on perspective. My perspective is that I could have started sooner, although I could be wrong. When do you think you started feeding your soul? Maybe you started very young or perhaps you haven't started yet. Either way, any of us can make the decision to start at any time. Start now. Start now. Start now. Stop everything you are doing and do something for your soul. Light your soul candle, spark the flame, and never allow it to go out.

Art will remain the most astonishing activity of mankind born out of struggle between wisdom and madness, between dream and reality in our mind.
-Magdalena Abakanwicz

Time to Grow

I hope you made the decision to find what feeds your soul and I hope that you acted on it. We only have a limited time in this life to do what we need to do and what we want to do for that matter. There isn't time for procrastination. To grow, we need to act. Acting is choosing to progress and to grow. Every day we are presented with choices and opportunities. Our free will allows us to make the decisions that guide us in the direction that we need to go in. Embrace your free will and let your intuition (gut) guide you. I promise you that your gut will not lead you in the wrong direction.

Your intuition is your soul's way of telling you things. Trust me, listen to it. It is never wrong. It is your truth. Once I realized this, my life definitely changed for the better. I wasn't finding myself stuck in uncomfortable situations any longer. We have all made decisions that we knew weren't right for us but because of pressure from others or other factors, we did it anyway. This never ends well. Even though we had that unsure feeling in our stomach, our brain did an override. Moving forward, try to listen to that feeling. You will be much happier and more successful if you do.

Intuition
Intuition, or gut feelings, can be thought of as the voice of our souls communicating to us. Whenever you feel drawn towards something or someone (without a fearful motive), you can be sure that this is your soul trying to guide you.

-Althenia Luna

What other things can we change in our lives to help our soul grow. Embracing all types of pure love is another growth aid. First of all, we need to have love and have respect for ourselves. We cannot start to love others until we do this. Many people really struggle with this concept. There are so many aspects of you to love. Some of these you may not even realize. Your flaws and mistakes are things that make you who you are. Embrace them with your whole heart. When you begin to realize that they create the uniqueness that is you, you can grow from them. Our mistakes are our daily lessons. Don't allow them to anger you. Let them grow your soul to new heights. The other types of love are a little more obvious to most of us. Make a point to display your love to family, friends, and even strangers. This is really very simple to do. Use words and actions to convey your love. The people that surround you should never wonder if they are loved by you. A simple "I love you" and a hug is all it takes. It will not only help with your soul growth, it will do wonders for theirs.

Finally, let your soul lead the way. Sometimes we don't realize that our soul knows exactly the right path to take. While our brain gets confused and caught up in decision making, our soul never experiences this. Because the soul is pure at its core, there is never a dilemma involved in where to go or what to do. A good way to think of it is in this way, your soul is the greatest GPS navigational system we could ask for and our brain is the vehicle. Allow your brain to drive and steer the car but always let your soul navigate the direction in which the car goes. If you do this, you will not be disappointed.

So remember, create, listen to your gut, love, and allow your soul to guide you. These are the pillars of your soul and the pathway to enlightenment. I cannot stress the importance of following this path. It can only lead to happiness and fulfillment. Isn't this what you want for yourself?

Awakening

You reach a point where you feel yourself going through an awakening. You look at what you used to do and who you used to be. It hurts because you realize you believed in and promoted nonsense. You grow; you evolve and you stop because you no longer operate at that frequency. As a result, there's certain people that you have to walk away from. As a result, you start to realize just how messed up the world is. You want to help; you want to heal; you want to make it a better world. This is how you know you're awakening a higher level of consciousness.

-Sylvester McNutt

Once you make the decision to live your life from the focal perspective of your soul, things will begin to change for you. Opportunities will begin to present themselves to you. The world will be opened up and be filled with unlimited possibilities. This is how your soul wants you to live your life. Believe in the knowledge within your true self and fulfill your soul's destiny. The faith that you possess in your soul will guide your future and lead you to happiness. If you have read this far in the book, I'm guessing that you have faith. You just have to make the decision.

The Tree

I'm not much of a fiction writer but I do have a story that I have written which I believe relates to the soul. It's a sort of short analogy story.

I once knew a man who was a tree farmer. He owned one of the largest tree farms in the entire area. He loved every tree that he had ever grown. Even though they all looked very similar, each were quite unique in their own way.

When he originally bought an enormous plot of land, he wasn't sure what he would do with it. He could build a large house on the land or he could use it to raise animals. Other people gave him their opinions on what they believed he should use his newly purchased land for. He thought and thought about what would be the most suitable use for the land.

One day, as he sat on a lone tree stump, it came to him. He realized there weren't any sources for trees in his area. "With all of this beautiful land, I will grow an amazing tree orchard. My land will produce the most amazing trees which I will sell to the world. I will help to make the world more beautiful. This farm will be the source of trees for this area."

The problem was that the man didn't know anything about growing trees. He would have to learn the science of the tree. He read books about trees and spoke to people who had knowledge on the subject of tree farming. He spent every waking moment doing this and finally he was ready.

He got his first bag of seeds. He dug many holes and placed a seed in each hole. The field was now filled with hopeful trees. He watered the trees and showered them with the love that they needed to grow big and strong. Within months, he began to see the trees poke up out of the dirt. As time passed, the trees began to form branches. Each branch was similar, yet very unique in its own right. Each tree was one source of energy but each branch took on its own individual path. Some would bend more than others or be longer than the others. They were each very distinct. He truly enjoyed watching the trees grow and form their own individuality.

New branches would constantly form and head in different directions. Sometimes branches would break off but the tree would always continue to grow. Each tree would live for a very long time. All the trees needed was water, sunlight, and the farmer's love. As *long as they had these necessities, they would grow and grow.*

The energy of each tree was never stifled. The harsh cold of the winter snow or the extreme heat of the summer sun would not stop the trees from growing and maturing. They each seemed to have a will that could not be broken.

When branches would fall off of the trees, the farmer would collect them and use them to burn at night in his fireplace. They would give him and his family warmth throughout the cold winter nights. In the summer months, he would use them for outdoor bonfires.

The farmer was always amazed when he returned to the tree that had lost branches. The tree always grew a new branch in the place of the old one. It was almost like the core energy of the tree knew it had to keep growing.

Like I said, fictional writing isn't my strong suit but I thought this pertained to the subject at hand. I thought about explaining the analogy but I think you get it.

The Constant of Inconsistency

Routine is definitely something created by the human mind. It helps us throughout our daily lives by establishing structure to our chaotic existence. I will be the first to admit to having many daily routines. I am, however, actively trying to let some of them go by substituting creative and spontaneous activities in their place. Having kids can happily lend to achieving this. Children do not seek and cling to routine like that of adults.

The human brain craves structure due to societal pressures. Naturally, our soul leans towards more creative and a less structured way of living, but from the moment we come into this life, pressure to be humanly "perfect" sways this. Like I have stated many times throughout this book, perfection is unnecessary and monotonously unfulfilling.

We live for a constant routine, when in fact, we should strive for an inconsistent and creative way of life. Routine does nothing for our soul. It actually has a way of causing our soul to go into a hibernation of sorts. When all we focus on is our daily routine, we are on auto-pilot. We aren't living our lives to their ultimate possibilities. We aren't experiencing life. It only benefits our mind. It is a stagnant way of getting from birth to death. Ideally, we can be responsible humans without being regimented in a routinely and conforming way of living. Conformity does not lead to creativity although responsibility does not challenge creativity. Shut your auto-pilot off and wake up your soul.

Living in the moment is a way of living a life of inconsistency. When I say inconsistency, I do not mean we should live a life of confusion, instability, or failure. It actually means living a life of spontaneity. It means being unconventional in some aspects of life. Spontaneous living lends itself to a creative lifestyle quite well. A "to-do-list" mentality is not a way to live. Like I said, this does not mean we should be lacking in responsibility. It just means that we should loosen our expectations on daily life. Also, loosen our stringent need to control our daily life.

Our soul needs to feel free, even when in the confines of a physical body. It is quite the conundrum for a soul, which has no physical attributes whatsoever, to be locked inside of a human body. Many individuals who have had a near death experience have stated how when they left their body, all of the physical weight and heaviness of human existence was gone. It is difficult for the soul to take on the weight of our daily lives. When our soul is with Source and not living a human life, it is weightless and free. There is no gravitational stress or expectations.

We need to try to be more constantly spontaneous and creative. We need to be spontaneously loving and in the moment. Let go of what you need to do and embrace what you want to do. We need to remind ourselves every day to live our lives this way. So many of us are stuck. Don't be stuck any longer. We can't change what has lacked in our past but we can change things so we aren't lacking in the future. Create your future because if you don't, nobody else will and stuck is what you will remain.

Who are the most spontaneous, creative, and loving humans on the planet? I'll give you a hint: we were all one once. The answer is children. Even though we were all children in our lives, we seem to forget this crucial stage in our existence. Children are pure. Purity equates to spontaneous creative love. When you are having a tough moment in your life, take a deep breath and remember back to being a kid. Think of a memorable and happy experience you had. I bet a smile will come to your face.

Why are children able to possess this level of purity? They simply are much closer to Source than adults are. Children were with Source not long ago. When they come into their earthly life, they have just exited their spirit life. They haven't been tainted by humanly and societal influences. It really makes you ask the question of a previous chapter, what if a child lived on an island with no outside contamination? They may stay in a pure state of being for their entire life.

Can you remember how you were as a child? Do you ever sit and reminisce about childhood moments? It's a healthy thing to do. If you can harness the emotional spontaneity of moments from childhood, we can remember that feeling and create those feelings as adults. Once we are capable of that, we can begin to change our perspective to be able to create our own creative way of living.

Once you can attain that childhood spontaneity, there is one other thing needed for true creativity. That would be inspiration. All art stems from some type of inspiration. We can be inspired by another artist, events happening around you or in the world, or the best possible inspiration, a dream. When we have a dream or a spark that appears in our soul which transpires into artistic inspiration, we can truly create. Many great artists have told stories of how they created masterpieces after it came to them in a dream. Here is a list of dream-inspired creations:

-#9 Dream by John Lennon
-Inception by Christopher Nolan
-Yesterday by The Beatles
-A majority of poetry by Edgar Allan Poe
-Dreamcatcher by Stephen King
-The Red Book by Carl Jung
-The Divine Comedy by Dante Alighieri
-Stuart Little by E.B. White
-The Sewing Machine
-Google
-Einstein's Theory of Relativity
-The shape of DNA
-The Periodic Table of Elements
-The Scientific Method

No matter where it comes from, inspiration is a key ingredient. Without inspiration, we would not have much.

To be more childlike, you don't have to give up being an adult. The fully integrated person is capable of being both an adult and a child simultaneously.

Recapture the childlike feelings of wide-eyed excitement, spontaneous appreciation, cutting loose, and being full of awe and wonder at this magnificent universe.

-Wayne Dyer

Love Your Creations

An artist is a humanly incarnation of a double-edged sword. Art of any type is created from the soul, yet all art is judged by the mind. It is analyzed and critiqued by something that has no business critiquing or criticizing the soul's creation. Can a computer explain the beauty of a sunset? Can a stereo speaker create beautiful music? Can a pen write amazing poetry on its own? No, No, and No. Just as these examples cannot happen, true art can only be accomplished by the soul.

An artist is a very ironic creature. They create from a place of purity but then tear it to pieces with the use of the mind. The mind's perspective is one of extreme harshness that has no derivative from the soul. How is it that you can create and then analyze? These are two completely contradictory actions. The ironic factor is that without our brain, our soul couldn't get the ideas out. An artist should create and then walk away, never to review the piece again.

True creation doesn't involve a fine toothed comb.

Even if a creation is flawed (which all art should be) it should hold a high level of value. To create is to appreciate. First of all, appreciate the action and guts that it takes to create and to send it out to the world. Secondly, view the creation from outside of your own perspective. Try to be an empathetic art critic. Lastly, love it because it was a creation that originated within a soul.

I have known many artists in my life. All of them, unless their arrogance got in the way, would create what I viewed as beautiful, yet they would think it was terrible. I once went to a friend's studio and looked at an incredible painting that he had done. The next week I returned to find that the canvas had been completely covered in white paint. I asked, what happened? He simply said, I hated it and I'm starting over. I truly did not understand, but that is the artistically, human mind. That is definitely not the soul talking. The soul would never erase the creation because it was created from purity and purity should never be erased.

I would love to hold a workshop for artists where they would create and never see their creation again. Artistic expression should never be erased. It should be sent out into the world to be witnessed and appreciated by everyone. To take back or revoke a work of art is a disservice to humanity. Imagine if Leonardo Davinci or Louis Armstrong or Martin Scorsese would have made the decision to not release their works to the world? We would be missing out on greatness because they didn't love what they created.

Interpretation is the revenge of the intellectual mind upon art. True works of art are like the infinity of the universe, you'll never enjoy them if you try to analyze them with your mind. Just appreciate them with your senses and allow them to seep into your soul.

-Me

Enjoy the Race

Life can be viewed as a metaphorical marathon if you will. Every day we get out of bed and put our running shoes on to complete another leg of our journey. For some of us, the race is a short one and for some it's much longer. Regardless of the number of years we live in each of our earthly lives, our goals are the same. Some people create and love more in a short amount of time than others do in one hundred years of life. We should stop looking at our lives in how many years we can sustain life, rather we should look at in a sense how much creative love did we produce.

Since we do live many lifetimes, we have numerous opportunities to accomplish our goals. Some of our lifetimes may be cut shorter than others but that's ok. There is a reason for every type of life we lead. Those soul contracts that I spoke of earlier are created for a purpose. That purpose is for learning. When a loved one passes over after a short life, it is extremely difficult but it teaches us about loss. It educates us by offering coping mechanisms. To cope is to live. As long as these coping mechanisms are not destructive or damaging, they are skills that grow our soul.

Another skill or mindset we can take away from loss is in the knowing that our loved one is not gone at all. Only their physical body is gone. Their soul, which is their true essence, is always with us. They may have moved on to another reality but they are always by our side. They are in a blissful state of existence. We should be happy for them, not sad for them. They are finally free of the earthly trials and tribulations. No more pain or stress is resting upon their shoulders. This, in my opinion, is the greatest lesson we can learn.

Each of us has our own race to finish. Every race has its own path. The directions in which we all go in are infinitely different. No one's race is the same. Some have a very smooth path while others' are full of bumps and potholes. Hopefully, it's not too smoothly paved. You may have just read that sentence and thought to yourself, that must have been a typo. It was not a typo. If a person's life is made "perfect" for them, they do not learn any important lessons. If an individual does not experience struggle and hardship, they do not learn. Life is full of daily struggle. The great Buddha taught that life is struggle and without it, there can be no progress. Removing this is a harmful and detrimental distortion of life. It will do nothing but harm a soul's truth.

Can you look back on your life and remember times of ease and times of struggle? Which of these moments were more educational and memorable? I would certainly guess that the hard times taught you much more. They made you stronger. They may have weakened you in the moment, but in the big picture of life, they built you up into a pillar of strength. With every moment of struggle that we experience, our pillar gets a little taller.

No one saves us but ourselves. No one can and no one may. We ourselves must walk the path.
-Buddha

The fact that you're struggling doesn't make you a burden. It doesn't make you unlovable or undesirable or undeserving of care. It doesn't make you too much or too sensitive or too needy. It makes you human.
-Daniell Koepke

The struggle you're in today is giving you the strength you need for tomorrow. Don't give up.
-Robert Tew

Tell Your Story

There is no greater agony than bearing an untold story inside of you.

-Maya Angelou

Now I understand that not everyone enjoys writing but it can be a very therapeutic pastime. Whether you write poetry, a book, or in a journal, it can be a process that helps release your feelings. Keeping our feelings locked within us can only lead to unhappiness. Many people don't have someone to share their feelings with or maybe they aren't comfortable talking about difficult things. Writing is an alternative option that can work for some people.

Maybe you are thinking, I am a terrible writer. There's no possible way that this is for me. The great thing about writing is that it's a creative process. This means that no matter what you write, it isn't wrong. Creativity is completely personal and subjective. Whatever you write is right. Don't worry about proper grammar or punctuation, just write. Write whatever comes to you. Just get it out.

Another great thing about writing is having something to leave behind. It can be comforting for our friends and loved ones to read our words when we are gone. I have heard many stories of people finding journals, letters, or poetry left behind by their loved ones. It is like a part of that person is on those pages and it feels like a direct connection from the living to their deceased loved one.

You can literally write about anything that is of interest to you. Obviously, expressing any harbored feelings is very important but using writing for creative expression can be just as beneficial. You may have a masterpiece inside of you that is just waiting to come out.

If writing just isn't something that is working for you, try another type of artistic expression. Is there something you have always wanted to try or possibly something artistic that you did when you were younger? Either way, make it happen as soon as possible. Again, there could be a masterpiece within you waiting to be released. Maybe it will only be appreciated by you or maybe it will be by the world. No matter how small or large the audience, this expression will benefit your soul more than you could ever imagine.

We need to tell our story. We all have a story that is only our own. A vision that only we can see from our own eyes and perspective. Nobody sees what we see and feels what we feel. Let others in on your perspective story. It is possible that your story could help someone else with their own story. You could benefit your own soul growth and someone else's also. Be an inspiration to yourself and to the world.

It's important that we share our experiences with other people. Your story will heal you and your story will heal somebody else. When you tell your story, you free yourself and give other people permission to acknowledge their own story.

-Iyanla Vanzant

Run Your Spiritual Gauntlet

Have you ever heard the expression, "throwing in the gauntlet?" It's an old saying that basically means a challenge. A similar expression was "running the gauntlet." This is an old military form of punishment in which the victim runs between two rows of men wearing armored gloves who beat him as he passes through the lines. Now, this is a very horrific image from barbaric times but it can be used as an analogy for our spiritual journey.

Our soul's journey is definitely not an easy one. It is filled with struggle, turmoil, and pain. It is also filled with joy, powerful lessons, and love. You cannot have love without pain, joy without struggle, or learning without turmoil; to have one without the other would lead to an unbalanced life. Sometimes it can be hard to realize these things amidst our daily lives. If we could take a moment every so often to step back, take a deep breath, and separate from our earthly chaos we would be able to see the bigger picture.

Every day we get hit with a metaphorical gauntlet. It takes the breath out of us and can knock us to the ground. We all experience this throughout our lives. We have the choice in how we deal with these knockdowns. This is where coping mechanisms come into play. You can crawl under a blanket and hide from the world and let the challenge hinder you or you can stare the challenge directly in the eye and overcome it. The choice is yours.

If we don't face our challenges of daily life and learn from them, our soul will have to repeat the challenges and lessons in another lifetime. These will have to be repeated until the lesson is learned. I recommend that every time you are confronted with a life lesson, you do everything in your power to soak up the lesson and learn it. Grow from it and become a greater person and therefore a greater soul because of it.

Your soul is a blank book filled with pages. These pages need to be filled with the lessons that lead our soul to enlightenment. There are many lessons to be learned and we spend as many lifetimes as we need to learn them. Enlightenment takes a very long time to accomplish. All great things take time to achieve.

The soul's true state of bliss (enlightenment) definitely takes the longest to achieve. Be conscious and respectful of the process and the mistakes that you will make along the way. As the saying goes, "all good things come to those who wait."

Honor Your Soul's Journey by Paying Attention to Your Intentions

May your journey be a conscious one where the intentions of your soul intersect with the intentions of your human nature on a daily basis, bringing both into alignment every moment of your life. That is what it means to experience heaven and earth.
-Dennis Merritt Jones

Your spiritual journey requires that you become emotionally aware, learn to make responsible choices, and use the ability to align your personality with your soul. Your intentions determine the trajectory of your life. If you are not aware of them, you follow a path that may lead you to places that you do not want to go. When you become aware of your emotions, learn to make responsible choices, and strive to create with the intentions of your soul, you encounter every part of your personality that opposes those intentions and are given the opportunity to challenge and change them

-Gary Zukav

Is it Time?

When it's our time to go, it's our time to go. We don't die by chance or coincidence. Why do some people die young and healthy while others die elderly and unhealthy? It's simple, we have a chosen time to pass on. Before each earthly incarnation, we agree to attempt to learn and teach certain lessons. Sometimes these lessons are for us and sometimes they are for others. It can be difficult to learn all the lessons necessary by ourselves. Death, and all of the aspects that are attached to it, is something that definitely can't be learned alone.

Losing a loved one is one of the hardest things we experience. Losing a loved one when they are a child or young adult is incomprehensible. We often ask ourselves, why would this happen? That person was so young and had so much life ahead of them. Well, I guarantee there was a specific reason for their passing. A lesson or many lessons can be found if you look for it. That individual had it written in their soul contract to pass early in life. This wasn't simply a coincidental death.

When someone passes, young or old, we grieve in our own unique way. Some people break down and cry for days while others put their grief into words on a page. However grief occurs, it is a painful process. After the initial grieving period ceases, we can begin to look for the lessons in the situation. I believe that many people never do this. It is a challenging thing to attempt, but it's a part of our purpose and process as a soul. To do this, we have to step back from the situation and view it from a learning perspective. When we are tangled up in the emotional turmoil of death, we can't see it objectively. Once we allow time to pass, this becomes much more probable.

Never attach guilt to someone's death. It was their time and nothing could have stopped that. So many people blame themself for another's passing, but there is no need or purpose for this. Everyone is going to die at some point. Once we begin to accept this and stop trying to control it, life can be a much happier and more beneficial experience.

Give yourself the opportunity to learn all that you can in this life and all that will follow. Make sure to always pay attention. Lessons can sometimes be hidden and not in plain sight.

They are gems that are so valuable for our soul's progression. A soul lesson is as precious as each breath we take in. Never forget to have appreciation for each and every one that presents itself to you.

The End of the Road
(not really)

Our lives are like the yellow brick road but instead of stretching from Kansas to Oz, it begins at birth and leads to death. The major difference in the two roads is that ours merely pauses at our physical death and begins again and again with each earthly life. Think of death as an intermission or a break from pain and struggle. During our intermission we are allowed to rest and reflect on our previous lifetime. We can be witness to how we helped and hurt others. Think of it as being an athlete and after the big game, being able to watch the game footage. We can review mistakes that were made and also see the great things that we did. This is an enormous learning experience.

How do we begin to prepare for the end of this road? Most people struggle with this certainty. Indeed, our physical death is a certainty. We all know that this is true yet many choose to ignore it. Not being able to have a conversation about death is like being unable to discuss any aspect of our reality. Physical death is a one-hundred percent factual occurrence for every human being yet most people have not found a means to cope with it. Coping is just the first step. The real issue is learning to accept it. Even bigger than acceptance is embracing it. Shouldn't we learn how to discuss it so we can accept, prepare, and embrace this fact? The answer is undeniably, yes.

The first step in acceptance of death is to realize that it is a peaceful experience. We have the idea that it will be a painful and scary time. This couldn't be more of an incorrect assumption. Dying is a painless transition from one existence to another. Think of death like a fresh and blissful beginning and not the end of anything.

This is one of my favorite Buddhist stories regarding death.

Buddha was staying in a village. A woman came to him, weeping and crying and screaming. Her child, her only child, had suddenly died. Because Buddha was in the village, people said, "Don't weep. Go to this man. People say he is infinite compassion. If he wills it, the child can revive. So don't weep. Go to this Buddha.

The woman came with the dead child, crying, weeping, and the whole village followed her- the whole village was affected. Buddha's disciples were also affected; they started praying in their minds that Buddha would have compassion. He must bless the child so that he will be revived, resurrected.

Many disciples of Buddha started weeping. The scene was so touching, deeply moving. Everybody was still. Buddha remained silent. He looked at the dead child, then he looked at the weeping, crying mother and he said to the mother, "Don't weep, just do one thing and your child will be alive again. Leave this dead child here, go back to the town, go to every house and ask every family if someone has ever died in their family, in their house. And if you can find a house where no one has ever died, then from them beg something to be eaten, some bread, some rice, or anything- but from the house where no one has ever died. And that bread or that rice will revive the child immediately. You go. Don't waste time."

The woman became happy. She felt that now the miracle was going to happen. She touched Buddha's feet and ran to the village which was not a very big one, very few cottages, a few families. She moved from one family to another, asking. But every family said, "This is impossible. There is not a single house- not only in this village but all over the earth- there is not a single house where no one has ever died, where people have not suffered deaths and the misery and the pain and the anguish that comes out of it.

By and by the woman realized that Buddha had been playing a trick. This was impossible. But still the hope was there. She went in asking until she had gone around the whole village. Her tears died, her hope died, but suddenly she felt a new tranquility, a serenity, coming to her. Now she realized that whosoever is born will have to die. It is only a question of years. Someone will die sooner, someone later but death is inevitable. She came back and touched Buddha's feet again and said to him, "As people say, you really do have a deep compassion for people."

-story source: The Book Of Secrets, by Osho

There are so many amazing lessons in this story. There is a lesson of the power of hope. There is the lesson of acceptance and obviously the lesson that death happens to everyone. We are not unique when it comes to physical death. However, it is probably the most personal thing that we will ever experience. Even though we think of it as not just about us, in actuality it is just about us. I don't mean that it is a selfish time, but death is our time for a transition.

Death is very similar to birth. In both, we are exiting one existence and entering another. There is one constant in both of these transitions, our soul. It always stays intact throughout both. Our soul propels our bodily vessel from birth to death. Actually, birth could be considered more difficult than death. I think we view birth differently due to the fact that there is hope and a future attached to it. The thing is, death also has hope and a future that accompanies it. It just looks a little different. Also, with birth, something is coming to us and not leaving us. Humans have trouble with the acceptance of losing physical things whether it be a meaningful material possession or a loved one. We thrive on things or people coming to us. The sunset in the rear view mirror is what we resist. The sunset is just as beautiful as the sunrise. Keep that in mind.

The second step in accepting death is realizing that we have to die to move on to a different life experience where we can learn new lessons. If we stayed in our current life forever, we would miss out on other life circumstances. There are so many factors that come into play when it comes to soul lessons. We need to experience different types of struggle and different types of love to grow. Imagine if you only were able to listen to one type of music for your entire life or read one book over and over. You wouldn't be very well versed in either music or literature. However, if you have access to a library or the radio, your outlook would be much different.

I truly hope that you walk away from this book with a different view of physical death. There is no need to fear it or be scared of it. Embrace life but also embrace the transition of death. Think about it and talk about it. Spread the message to accept death and the positivity of what our soul is meant to do. We need to have appreciation for every minute we are on this earth. We also need to have appreciation for the other side in which we pass. There is great knowledge for our soul on both sides. Without one, the other is pointless and without both we are not a complete soul.

The Beginning at the End of the Path

The majority of this book has been about our soul's earthly physical life. I want to conclude all of this with my view of what happens when we leave our physicality.

As humans, we have a checklist of sorts. We equate our happiness to checking the boxes that we think make us happy. When I say this, I mean our mind has a list that entails what we think will make us happy. We have a preconceived notion of what our life should look like. These are unrealistic expectations that seldom materialize.

There is no factual proof to this final chapter. It is being written from my soul's faithful perspective. This will be an abstractly and objectively bookend to this life. It is somewhat simple to write about a life that we are currently living. It is yet another to write about an existence that has been covered by a veil. An existence that my soul knows but my mind does not. An existence that your soul also knows but your mind does not. I am speaking of our soul's experience between our earthly lives.

When our body ceases to exist, our soul moves on into bliss. This is a happiness that is difficult to put into words. It is pure and free from human pain and stress. Hard to imagine isn't it? Our mind cannot easily conceptualize this. That is okay because our mind has nothing to do with this time in our existence.

When we pass over, everything of material value that we are leaving behind does not come with us. Our soul will however stay connected with the loved ones we have left behind because our soul is connected to their souls. All of our human concerns do not follow us. When our brain ceases to exist, anything that our brain was attached to ceases to exist. Concerns cease to exist. We are finally free. Free from pain, free from worry, and free from disappointment. This is why I use the word, bliss.

What are some things about your earthly life that make you unhappy? I guarantee that any answer you give doesn't exist when we pass over. Sounds pretty good, doesn't it? I believe it does. Our soul doesn't feel the unhappiness on the other side that we feel when we are in human existence.

When our soul is on the other side, it creates an environment that resonates with its truth. Our soul's truth is whatever makes it feel fulfilled. Whatever makes your soul feel fulfilled when you are on earth, that will be what your soul creates after death. When we return to Source, we create our own unique "happy place." Close your eyes and imagine your "happy place." This will be the place that you live in when you pass over. I have a few " happy places" that I believe will be where my soul resides.

When we reach the other side, our relationships with other souls are unconditionally loving. All souls love each other without judgement. If you have children, you can relate to this feeling of unconditional love. Imagine having this same feeling for everyone. It would be remarkable and could possibly make our planet a much healthier and more positive place to live.

Back to how our soul's existence looks when we pass over. It creates whatever makes it happy. I love the idea of playing drums on an outdoor stage while it's snowing and my kids are with me. I also embrace sitting at a computer on a sunny morning and typing my most creative thoughts. Basically, any environment where I have my kids and my creativity. That is my heaven. Throw in some snow and I will be ecstatic. What is your heaven? We all know what it is. We just need to realize that this is what awaits us when we leave this life.

For me personally, one major thing that I look forward to the most when I am on the other side is having a relationship. Not a parental relationship or a family one. I am talking about a soulmate relationship like the one I had in my earthly life but without all of the superficial expectations that accompanied it. I am speaking about two souls that coexist within the bliss. This could be the final piece that completes my soul's infinite circle.

What will be something or things that will complete your soul's infinite circle?

Epilogue

Life isn't about the destination, it's about the journey. The journey is the anticipation of the destination and when it comes to our soul, the journey is a lengthy one. It is a road paved with creativity, pain, love, and struggle. It is speed bumps and potholes lit by a rainbow of opportunities. We need to accept the good with the bad and learn to appreciate the balance of our existence. We travel from lifetime to lifetime within the human vessel learning the lessons needed to progress. The lessons are rooted in love and creativity and they are all we need.

Wake each day with glorious happiness and respect for the time we are given in each lifetime. Whether it's a few years or one hundred, love and live every moment to its full potential. Challenge yourself by being as creative and loving as you can be. The thing is, it's not a challenge at all. It's a simplicity that comes completely natural to our soul. All you need is to embrace the creativity that naturally flows within you. Embrace it and let it out. It's beauty will transcend you to places you could never imagine simply with your mind.

Your soul is something of an anomaly. It is not normal or expected. It is not stagnant or mundane. It is a spontaneous eruption of artistic genius. The soul can craft other-worldly inventions that the mind solely could not. The mind transcribes what the soul is creating but the soul is always steering the ship. Always allow it to steer and guide your way. If you do, you will never be disappointed.

The soul is the captain and the captain always leads the journey. If your ego can step aside and allow the captain to lead, you will always reach the horizon. You will become one with the sun as it sets upon the earth. You will become one with your true self.

-Me